SEVENTH EDITION

FLASHMAPS
NEW YORK

Editorial Updater
Andrew Collins

Cartographic Updater
Bello Design

Proofreader
Tim Reynolds

Editor
Robert Blake

Cover Design
Guido Caroti

Creative Director
Fabrizio La Rocca

Cartographer
David Lindroth

Designer
Tigist Getachew

Cartographic Contributors
Edward Faherty
Sheila Levin
Page Lindroth
Marcy S. Pritchard
Eric Rudolph

Fodor's   www.fodors.com

Fodor's Travel Publications · New York, Toronto, London, Sydney, Auckland

Special Sales

Fodor's Travel Publications are available at special discounts for bulk purchases for sales promotions or premiums. Special editions, including personalized covers, excerpts of existing guides, and corporate imprints, can be created in large quantities for special needs. For more information, contact your local bookseller or write to Special Markets, Fodor's Travel Publications, 1745 Broadway, New York, NY 10019. Inquiries from Canada should be directed to your local Canadian bookseller or sent to Random House of Canada, Ltd., Marketing Dept., 2775 Matheson Blvd. East, Mississauga, Ontario L4W 4P7. Inquiries from the United Kingdom should be sent to Fodor's Travel Publications, 20 Vauxhall Bridge Rd., London SW1V 2SA, England. **ISBN 1-4000-1206-6** **ISSN 1527-4853**

PRINTED IN GERMANY 10 9 8 7 6 5 4 3 2 1

Area Codes: Manhattan (212, 646, 917); Bronx, Brooklyn, Queens, Staten Island (718, 347); Nassau/Suffolk (516); Northern NJ (201, 973). All (212) unless otherwise noted.

EMERGENCIES

AAA Emergency Road Service ☎ 800/222-4357

Ambulance, Fire, Police ☎ 911

Animal Bites ☎ 676-2483

Animal Medical Center ☎ 838-8100

Arson Hotline ☎ 800/FIRE-TIP

Child Abuse ☎ 800/342-3720

Crime Victim Hotline ☎ 577-7777

Domestic Violence Hotline ☎ 800/621-HOPE

Drug Abuse ☎ 800/395-3400

Lesbian and Gay Anti-Violence Project ☎ 714-1184

Mental Health Crisis Hotline/LifeNet ☎ 800/543-3638

Park Emergencies ☎ 800/201-7275

Poison Control ☎ 340-4494

Rape Hotline ☎ 800/656-4673

Runaway Hotline ☎ 800/621-4000

Sexual Assualt Reports ☎ 267-7273

Suicide Prevention ☎ 673-3000

SERVICES

AAA ☎ 757-2000

AIDS Hotline (CDC) ☎ 800/342-2437

AIDS Hotline (NY) ☎ 800/541-AIDS

Alcoholics Anonymous ☎ 870-3400

Amex Lost Travelers Checks ☎ 800/221-7282

ASPCA ☎ 876-7700

Better Business Bureau ☎ 533-6200

Big Apple Greeters ☎ 669-2896

Chamber of Commerce ☎ 493-7400

Convention & Visitor's Bureau ☎ 484-1200

Dept of Aging ☎ 442-1000

Dept of Consumer Affairs ☎ 487-4444

Dept of Health ☎ 442-9666

Dept of Sanitation ☎ 219-8090

Dept of Transportation ☎ 768-4653

Housing Authority ☎ 306-3000

HRA Infoline ☎ 877/472-8411

Immigration and Naturalization Service ☎ 800/375-5283

Legal Aid Society ☎ 577-3300

Lesbian & Gay Community Service Center ☎ 620-7310

Mayor's Office ☎ 788-7585

Mayor's Office for People With Disabilities ☎ 788-2830

Medicare ☎ 800/638-6833

NY Post Office ☎ 967-8585

NY Public Library Telephone Reference Service ☎ 340-0849

Overeaters Anonymous ☎ 206-8621

Passport Information ☎ 206-3500

Planned Parenthood ☎ 274-7200

Social Security ☎ 800/772-1213

Taxi Complaints ☎ 302-8294

Towaways ☎ 869-2929

Traffic Information ☎ 787-3387

Traveler's Aid ☎ 718/656-4870

24-Hour Locksmith ☎ 247-6747

UN Information ☎ 963-1234

US Customs ☎ 800/697-3662

TOURS

Adventure on a Shoestring ☎ 265-2663

Art Tours ☎ 239-4160

Bateaux New York ☎ 352-2022

Big Onion Walking Tours ☎ 439-1090

Central Park Bike Tours ☎ 541-8759

Circle Line ☎ 563-3200

Doorways to Design ☎ 718/339-1542

Dr. Phil's NY Talks and Walks ☎ 888/377-4455

Gray Line ☎ 397-2600

Helicopter Flight Services ☎ 355-0801

Joyce Gold History Tours ☎ 242-5762

Liberty Helicopter ☎ 465-8905

Municipal Art Society ☎ 935-3960

NY Waterway Ferries ☎ 800/53-FERRY

NYC Cultural Walking Tours ☎ 979-2388

NYC Discovery Walking Tours ☎ 465-3331

Radical Walking Tours ☎ 718/492-0069

Rockefeller Center Tour ☎ 664-3700

Spirit Cruises of NY ☎ 727-2789

UN Tours ☎ 963-8687

World Yacht Cruises ☎ 630-8100

PARKS AND RECREATION

Acqueduct & Belmont Race Tracks
☎ 718/641-4700

Central Park Boat Rental ☎ 517-2233

Continental Arena ☎ 201/935-3900

Empire Skate Club ☎ 774-1774

Five Borough Bicycle Club
☎ 932-2300

Giants Stadium ☎ 201/935-8222

Jets Information ☎ 516/560-8200

Madison Square Garden
☎ 465-6741

Meadowlands Box Office
☎ 201/935-3900

Meadowlands Race Track
☎ 201/935-8500

Nassau Coliseum ☎ 516/794-9300

NY Botanic Garden ☎ 718/817-1700

NY Islanders ☎ 516/794-4100

NY Knicks ☎ 465-5867

NY Mets ☎ 718/507-8499

NY Road Runners ☎ 860-2280

NY Yankees ☎ 718/293-6000

Parks Events ☎ 888/NY-PARKS

Shea Stadium ☎ 718/507-6387

US Open Tennis ☎ 718/760-6200

Yankee Stadium Tours
☎ 718/579-4531

Yonkers Raceway ☎ 914/968-4200

Zoo/Bronx ☎ 718/367-1010

Zoo/Central Park ☎ 861-6030

TRANSPORTATION

Access-a-Ride ☎ 877/337-2017

Airport Travel Info ☎ 800/AIR-RIDE

Amtrak ☎ 800/872-7245

Bonanza Bus Lines ☎ 800/556-3815

Bus & Subway Accessibility
☎ 718/596-8585

Bus & Subway Customer Service
☎ 718/330-3322

Bus & Subway Information
☎ 718/330-1234

Bus & Subway Service Status
☎ 718/243-7777

Ellis Island/Statue of Liberty Ferry
☎ 269-5755

EZ Pass Information
☎ 800/333-8655

Fire Island Ferries ☎ 631/665-3600

Greyhound Bus Lines
☎ 800/231-2222

JFK Airport ☎ 718/244-4444

La Guardia Airport ☎ 718/533-3400

Long Island Railroad (LIRR)
☎ 718/217-5477

Martz Trailways ☎ 800/233-8604

Metro-North ☎ 532-4900;
800/METRO-INFO

NJ Transit ☎ 800/626-7433;
973/762-5100

NY Airport Service ☎ 718/875-8200

NY Waterway Ferries
☎ 800/53-FERRY

Newark Airport ☎ 973/961-6000

Olympia Airport Express
☎ 877/894-9155

Passenger Ship Terminal
☎ 246-5451

PATH ☎ 800/234-7284

Peter Pan Trailways
☎ 800/343-9999

Port Authority Bus Information
☎ 564-8484

Roosevelt Island Tram ☎ 832-4543

SeaStreak Ferry ☎ 800/262-8743

Short Line ☎ 800/631-8405

Staten Island Ferry ☎ 718/815-2628

SuperShuttle ☎ BLUE-VAN

Trailways ☎ 800/858-8555

**Triborough Bridge and Tunnel
Authority** ☎ 360-3000

Vermont Transit ☎ 800/451-3292

ENTERTAINMENT

Big Apple Circus ☎ 268-2500

Broadway Line ☎ 302-4111

Carnegie Hall ☎ 247-7800

Central Park Summerstage
☎ 360-2777

City Tix ☎ 581-1212

Historic House Museums
☎ 360-8282

Jazz Line ☎ 479-7888

Lincoln Center ☎ 546-2656

Movie Phone ☎ 777-FILM

NYC On Stage ☎ 768-1818

Radio City Music Hall ☎ 247-4777

**Reduced Price Theatre Tickets
(TKTS)** ☎ 768-1818

**Shakespeare in the Park/Delacorte
Theater** ☎ 861-7283

Telecharge ☎ 239-6200

Ticket Central ☎ 279-4200

Ticketmaster ☎ 307-7171

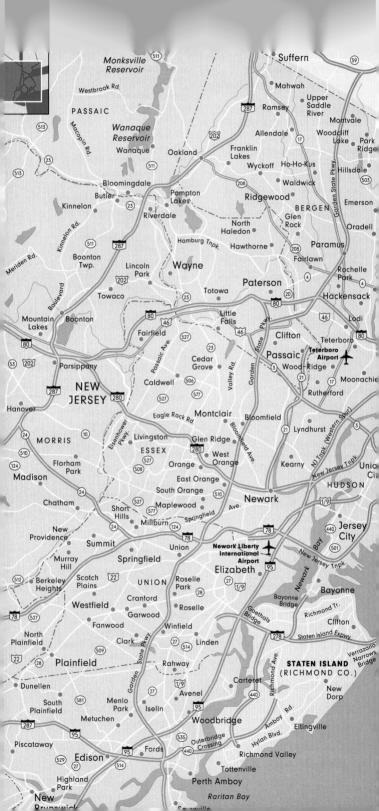

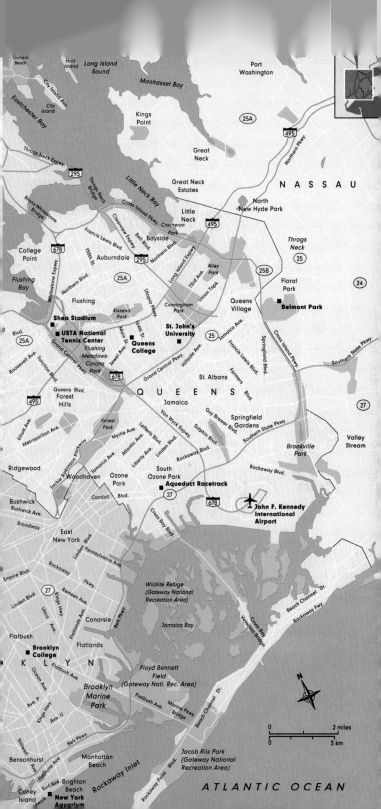

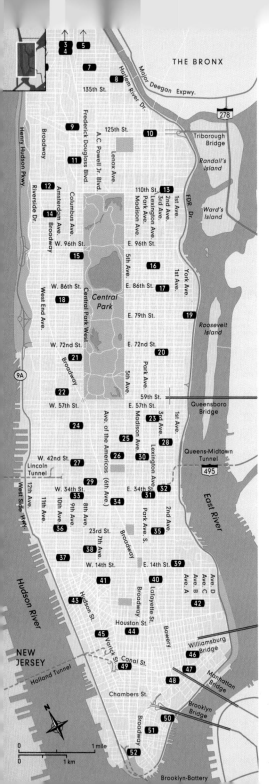

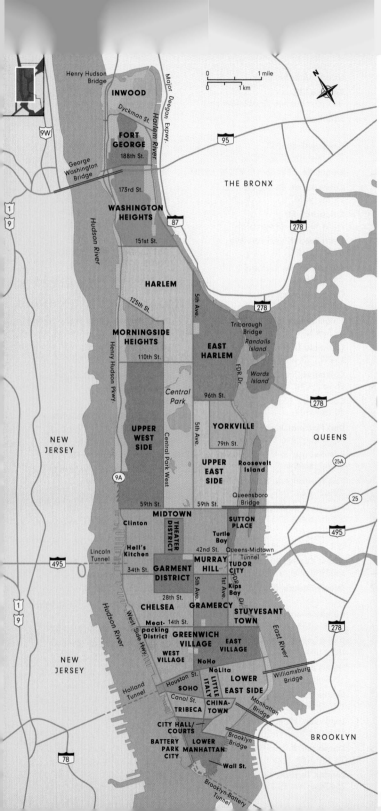

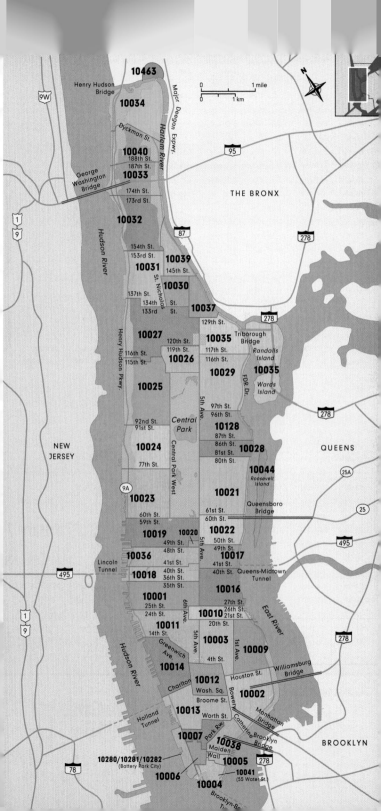

Streets	West End Ave.	Broadway	Amsterdam Ave.	Columbus Ave.	Central Park West
94–96	700-737	2520-2554	702-733	701-740	350-360
92–94	660-699	2476-2519	656-701	661-700	322-336
90–92	620-659	2440-2475	620-655	621-660	300-320
88–90	578-619	2401-2439	580-619	581-620	279-295
86–88	540-577	2361-2400	540-579	541-580	262-275
84–86	500-539	2321-2360	500-539	501-540	241-257
82–84	460-499	2281-2320	460-499	461-500	212-239
80–82	420-459	2241-2280	420-459	421-460	211 American Museum of Natural History
78–80	380-419	2201-2240	380-419	381-420	
76–78	340-379	2161-2200	340-379	341-380	
74–76	300-339	2121-2160	300-339	301-340	145-160
72–74	262-299	2081-2114	261-299	261-300	121-135
70–72	221-261	2040-2079	221-260	221-260	101-115
68–70	176-220	1999-2030	181-220	181-220	80-99
66–68	122-175	1961-1998	140-180	141-180	65-79
64–66	74-121	1920-1960	100-139	101-140	50-55
62–64	44-73	Lincoln Center	60-99	61-100	25-33
60–62	20-43	1841-1880	20-59	21-60	15
58–60	2-19	Columbus Circle	1-19	2-20	Columbus Circle

	11th Ave.	Broadway	10th Ave.	9th Ave.	8th Ave.	7th Ave.	6th Ave.
56–58	823-854	1752-1791	852-889	864-907	946-992	888-921	1381-1419
54–56	775-822	1710-1751	812-851	824-863	908-945	842-887	1341-1377
52–54	741-774	1674-1709	772-811	782-823	870-907	798-841	1301-1330
50–52	701-740	1634-1673	737-770	742-781	830-869	761-797	1261-1297
48–50	665-700	1596-1633	686-735	702-741	791-829	720-760	1221-1260
46–48	625-664	1551-1595	654-685	662-701	735-790	701-719	1180-1217
44–46	589-624	1514-1550	614-653	622-661	701-734	Times Square	1141-1178
42–44	553-588	1472-1513	576-613	582-621	661-700		1100-1140
40–42	503-552	1440-1471	538-575	Port Authority	620-660	560-598	1061-1097
38–40	480-502	1400-1439	502-537		570-619	522-559	1020-1060
36–38	431-471	1352-1399	466-501	468-501	520-569	482-521	981-1019
34–36	405-430	Macy's	430-465	432-467	480-519	442-481	Herald Square
32–34	360-404	1260-1282	380-429	412-431	442-479	Penn Station	
30–32	319-359	1220-1279	341-379	Post Office	403-441	362-399	855-892
28–30	282-318	1178-1219	314-340	314-351	362-402	322-361	815-844
26–28	242-281	1135-1177	288-313	262-313	321-361	282-321	775-814
24–26	202-241	1100-1134	239-287	230-261	281-320	244-281	733-774
22–24	162-201	940-1099	210-238	198-229	236-280	210-243	696-732
20–22	120-161	902-939	162-209	167-197	198-235	170-209	656-695
18–20	82-119	873-901	130-161	128-166	162-197	134-169	613-655
16–18	54-81	860-872	92-129	92-127	126-161	100-133	574-612
14–16	26-53	Union Square	58-91	44-91	80-125	64-99	530-573

Crosstown Street Address Finder

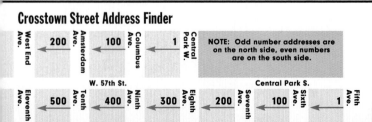

West End Ave. → 200 → Amsterdam Ave. → 100 → Columbus Ave. → 1 → Central Park W.

NOTE: Odd number addresses are on the north side, even numbers are on the south side.

W. 57th St.

Eleventh Ave. → 500 → Tenth Ave. → 400 → Ninth Ave. → 300 → Eighth Ave. → 200 → Seventh Ave. → 100 → Sixth Ave. → 1 → Fifth Ave.

Central Park S.

Central Park

5th Ave.	Madison Ave.	Park Ave.	Lexington Ave.	3rd Ave.	2nd Ave.	1st Ave.	Streets
1130–1148	1340–1379	1199–1236	1449–1486	1678–1709	1817–1868	1817–1855	**94–96**
1109–1125	1295–1335	1160–1192	1400–1444	1644–1677	1766–1808	1780–1811	**92–94**
1090–1107	1254–1294	1120–1155	1361–1396	1601–1643	1736–1763	1740–1779	**90–92**
1070–1089	1220–1250	1080–1114	1311–1355	1568–1602	1700–1739	1701–1735	**88–90**
1050–1069	1178–1221	1044–1076	1280–1301	1530–1566	1660–1698	1652–1689	**86–88**
1030–1048	1130–1171	1000–1035	1248–1278	1490–1529	1624–1659	1618–1651	**84–86**
1010–1028	1090–1128	960–993	1210–1248	1450–1489	1584–1623	1578–1617	**82–84**
990–1009	1058–1088	916–959	1164–1209	1410–1449	1538–1583	1540–1577	**80–82**
970–989	1012–1046	878–911	1120–1161	1374–1409	1498–1537	1495–1539	**78–80**
950–969	974–1006	840–877	1080–1116	1330–1373	1456–1497	1462–1494	**76–78**
930–947	940–970	799–830	1036–1071	1290–1329	1420–1454	1429–1460	**74–76**
910–929	896–939	760–791	1004–1032	1250–1289	1389–1417	1344–1384	**72–74**
895–907	856–872	720–755	962–993	1210–1249	1328–1363	1306–1343	**70–72**
870–885	813–850	680–715	926–961	1166–1208	1296–1327	1266–1300	**68–70**
850–860	772–811	640–679	900–922	1130–1165	1260–1295	1222–1260	**66–68**
830–849	733–771	600–639	841–886	1084–1129	1222–1259	1168–1221	**64–66**
810–828	690–727	560–599	803–842	1050–1083	1180–1221	1130–1167	**62–64**
790–807	654–680	520–559	770–802	1010–1049	1140–1197	1102–1129	**60–62**
755–789	621–649	476–519	722–759	972–1009	Queensborough Bridge		**58–60**
720–754	572–611	434–475	677–721	942–968	1066–1101	1026–1063	**56–58**
680–719	532–568	408–430	636–665	894–933	1028–1062	985–1021	**54–56**
656–679	500–531	360–399	596–629	856–893	984–1027	945–984	**52–54**
626–655	452–488	320–350	556–593	818–855	944–983	889–944	**50–52**
600–625	412–444	280–300	518–555	776–817	902–943	860–888	**48–50**
562–599	377–400	240–277	476–515	741–775	862–891	827	**46–48**
530–561	346–375	Met Life (200)	441–475	702–735	824–860	785	United Nations **44–46**
500–529	316–345	Grand Central	395–435	660–701	793–823		**42–44**
460–499	284–315		354–394	622–659	746–773	Tudor City	**40–42**
424–459	250–283	68–99	314–353	578–621	707–747	666–701	**38–40**
392–423	218–249	40–67	284–311	542–577	666–700	Midtown Tunnel	**36–38**
352–391	188–217	5–35	240–283	508–541	622–659	599–626	**34–36**
320–351	152–184	1–4	196–239	470–507	585–621	556–598	**32–34**
284–319	118–150	444–470	160–195	432–469	543–581	Kips Bay	**30–32**
250–283	79–117	404–431	120–159	394–431	500–541	NYU Hosp.	**28–30**
213–249	50–78	364–403	81–119	358–393	462–499	446–478	**26–28**
201–212	11–37	323–361	40–77	321–355	422–461	411–445	**24–26**
172–200	1–7	286–322	9–39	282–318	382–421	390–410	**22–24**
154–170		251–285	1–8	244–281	344–381	315–389	**20–22**
109–153		221–250	70–78	206–243	310–343	310–314	**18–20**
85–127		184–220	40–69	166–205	301–309	280–309	**16–18**
69–108		Union Square	2–30	126–165	230–240	240–279	**14–16**

Park Ave. · Park Ave. S. · Lexington Ave. · Irving Pl.

Fifth Ave. | Madison Ave. | Park Ave. | Lexington Ave. | Third Ave. | Second Ave. | First Ave.

1 →   100 →   140 →   200 →   300 →   400 →

Letter codes refer to grid sectors on preceding map

Abingdon Sq. B1
Albany St. B6, C5
Allen St. D2, D3
Ann St. C5, D5
Astor Pl. D1
Attorney St. E2
Ave. A E1, E2
Ave. B E1, E2
Ave. C E1, E2
Ave. D E1, E2
Ave. of the Americas (Sixth Ave.) C1, C4
Bank St. A2, B1
Barclay St. C5
Barrow St. B2
Baruch Pl. F2
Battery Pl. C6
Baxter St. D3, D4
Bayard St. D4
Beach St. B4
Beaver St. C6, D6
Bedford St. B2, C2
Beekman St. D5
Bethune St. A1, B1
Bleecker St. B1, D2
Bond St. D2
Bowery D2, D4
Bowling Green C6
Bridge St. C6, D6
Broadway C1, C6
Brooklyn Battery Tunnel C6, D6
Brooklyn Bridge D5, F5
Broome St. B3, E3
Burling Slip D5
Canal St. C3, E3
Cardinal Hayes Plaza D4
Carlisle St. C6
Carmine St. B2
Catherine La. C4
Catherine Slip E4
Catherine St. D4, E4
Cedar St. C5, D5
Central Market D3
Centre St. D3, D5
Chambers St. B4, D4
Charles St. B1, B2

Charlton St. B3, C3
Chatham Sq. D4
Cherry St. E4, F3
Christopher St. B2, C1
Chrystie St. D2, D3
Church St. C4, C5
Clarkson St. B2, B3
Cleveland Pl. D3
Clinton St. E2, E4
Coenties Slip D6
Columbia St. E2, E3
Commerce St. B2
Cooper Sq. D1, D2
Cornelia St. B2
Cortlandt St. C5
Crosby St. C2, C3
Delancey St. D3, E3
Depyster St. D6
Desbrosses St. B3
Dey St. C5
Division St. D4, E4
Dominick St. B3, C3
Dover St. D5
Downing St. B2, C2
Doyers St. D4
Duane St. C4, D4
East Broadway D4, E3
East Houston St. D2, F2
East River Drive F1, F3
East Washington Pl. C2
Eighth Ave. B1
Eldridge St. D2, D3
Elizabeth St. D2, D4
Elk St. D4
Ericsson Pl. C4
Essex St. E2, E3
Exchange Pl. C6, D6
Father Demo Sq. C2
FDR Dr. F1, F3
Federal Plaza C4, D4
Fifth Ave. C1
First Ave. D1, D2
Fletcher St. D5
Foley Sq. D4
Forsyth St. D4, E4
Fourth Ave. D1
Franklin St. C4

Front St. D6
Fulton St. C5, D5
Gansevoort St. A1, B1
Gay St. B1, C1
Gold St. D5
Gouverneur La. D6
Gouverneur St. E3
Grand St. C3, F3
Great Jones St. D2
Greene St. C1, C3
Greenwich Ave. B1, C1
Greenwich St. B1, C6
Grove St. B2
Hanover Sq. D6
Hanover St. D6
Harrison St. B4, C4
Henry St. D4, E3
Hester St. D3, E3
Hogan Pl. D4
Holland Tunnel A4, C3
Horatio St. A1, B1
Hubert St. B4
Hudson St. B1, C4
Independence Plaza B4, C4
Jackson St. F3
James St. D4
Jane St. A1, B1
Jay St. C4
Jefferson St. E3
John St. C5, D5
Jones Alley D2
Jones St. B2
Kenmare St. D3
Kent Pl. D4
King St. B3, C3
Lafayette St. D1, D4
LaGuardia Pl. C2
Laight St. B4
Leonard St. C4
Leroy St. B2
Lewis St. F3
Liberty St. C5
Lispenard St. C4
Little W. 12th St. A1
Ludlow St. E2, E3
MacDougal Alley C1
MacDougal St. C1, C3

MAP 8
Hospitals & Late-Night Pharmacies

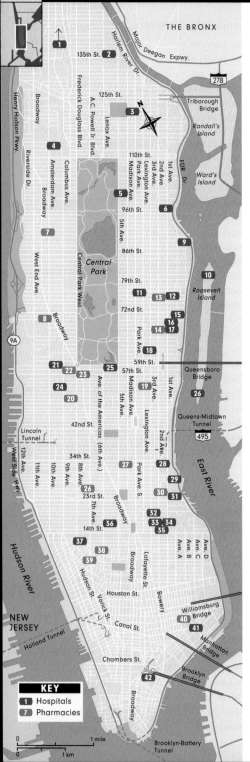

KEY
1 Hospitals
7 Pharmacies

Listed Alphabetically

HOSPITALS

Bellevue Hospital Center, 29.
462 First Ave ☎ 562–4141

Beth Israel Med Center, 34.
First Ave at 16th St ☎ 420–2000

Beth Israel Singer Division, 9.
170 East End Ave ☎ 870-9000

Cabrini Med Center, 32. 227 E 19th St
☎ 995–6000

Coler-Goldwater Memorial, 10.
900 Main St, Roosevelt Island
☎ 848–6300

Coler-Goldwater Memorial, 26.
1 Main St, Roosevelt Island
☎ 318–8000

Columbia–Presbyterian Med Ctr, 1.
622 W 168th St ☎ 305-2500

Gouverneur, 41. 227 Madison St
☎ 238–7000

Gracie Square (Psychiatric), 12.
420 E 76th St ☎ 988–4400

Harlem Hospital Center, 2.
506 Lenox Ave ☎ 939–1000

Joint Diseases, 33. 301 E 17th St
☎ 598–6000

Lenox Hill, 11. 100 E 77th St
☎ 439–2345

Manhattan Eye, Ear, & Throat, 18.
210 E 64th St ☎ 838–9200

Memorial Sloan-Kettering (Cancer), 17. 1275 York Ave ☎ 639–7203

Metropolitan, 6. 1901 First Ave
☎ 423–6262

Mount Sinai, 5. Fifth Ave at 100th St
☎ 241–6500

New York Cornell Med Center, 16.
525 E 68th St ☎ 746–5454

New York Eye & Ear, 35. 310 E 14th St
☎ 979–4000

New York Foundling (Children), 36.
590 Sixth Ave ☎ 633–9300

North General, 3.
Madison Ave at 123rd St ☎ 429–4000

NY Harbor/VA Hospital, 31.
408 First Ave ☎ 686–7500

NYU Downtown, 42.
170 William St ☎ 312–5000

NYU Med Center, 28. 550 First Ave
☎ 374–4000

Payne Whitney (Psychiatric), 12.
525 E 68th St ☎ 746–5700

Special Surgery, 15. 535 E 70th St
☎ 606–1000

St Clare's, 24. 415 W 51st St
☎ 586–1500

St Luke's–Roosevelt, 4.
1111 Amsterdam Ave ☎ 523–4000

St Luke's–Roosevelt, 21.
428 W. 59th St ☎ 523–4000

St Vincent's, 37. 153 W 11th St
☎ 604–7000

LATE–NIGHT/24-HOUR PHARMACIES

Apthorp Pharmacy, 8.
2201 Broadway ☎ 800/775-3582

Bigelow Pharmacy, 38.
414 Sixth Ave ☎ 533–2700

CVS Pharmacy, 19.
630 Lexington Ave ☎ 917/369–8688
(24-hour)

CVS Pharmacy, 30. 342 E 23rd St
☎ 505–1555 (24-hour)

CVS Pharmacy, 22. 400 W. 59th St
☎ 245–0617 (24-hour)

Duane Reade, 7. 2465 Broadway
☎ 799–3172 (24-hour)

Duane Reade, 13. 1279 Third Ave
☎ 744–2668 (24-hour)

Duane Reade, 23. 224 W. 57th St
☎ 541–9708 (24-hour)

Genovese, 14. 1299 Second Ave
☎ 772–0104

Metropolis Drug Co, 25.
721 Ninth Ave ☎ 246–0168

Rite Aid, 20. 303 W. 50th St
☎ 247–8384 (24-hour)

Rite Aid, 40. 408 Grand St
☎ 529–7115 (24-hour)

Village Apothecary, 39.
346 Bleecker St ☎ 807–7566

Walgreens, 27.
350 Fifth Ave ☎ 868–5659 (24-hour)

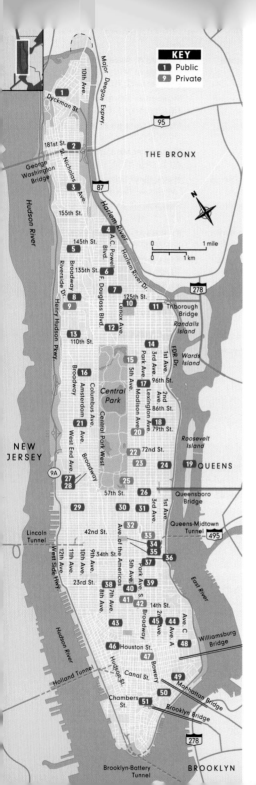

KEY
1 Public
9 Private

Listed Alphabetically

CONSULATES

Afghanistan, 93. 360 Lexington Ave ☎ 972-1212

Argentina, 23. 12 W 56th St ☎ 603-0400

Australia, 75. 150 E 42nd St ☎ 351-6500

Austria, 11. 31 E 69th St ☎ 737-6400

Bahamas, 53. 231 E 46th St ☎ 421-6420

Bahrain, 64. 2 UN Plaza, E 44th St ☎ 888-1552

Bangladesh, 68. 211 E 43rd St ☎ 599-6767

Barbados, 71. 800 Second Ave ☎ 867-8435

Belarus, 52. 708 third Ave ☎ 682-5392

Belgium, 33. 1330 Sixth Ave ☎ 586-5110

Bhutan, 64. 2 UN Plaza ☎ 826-1919

Bolivia, 68. 211 E 43rd St ☎ 687-0530

Brazil, 29. 1185 Sixth Ave ☎ 917/777-7777

Bulgaria, 18. 121 E. 62nd St ☎ 935-4646

Canada, 36. 1251 Sixth Ave ☎ 596-1628

Chile, 41. 866 UN Plaza ☎ 980-3366

China, 97. 520 Twelfth Ave ☎ 279-4275

Colombia, 56. 10 E 46th St ☎ 949-9898

Costa Rica, 101. 80 Wall St ☎ 425-2620

Croatia, 92. 369 Lexington Ave ☎ 599-3066

Cyprus, 94. 13 E 40th St ☎ 686-6016

Czech Republic, 2. 1109 Madison Ave ☎ 717-5643

Denmark, 49. 885 Second Ave ☎ 223-4545

Dominican Republic, 58. 1501 Broadway ☎ 768-2480

Ecuador, 71. 800 Second Ave ☎ 808-0170

Egypt, 20. 1110 Second Ave ☎ 759-7120

El Salvador, 90. 46 Park Ave ☎ 889-3608

Estonia, 79. 600 Third Ave ☎ 883-0636

Finland, 41. 866 UN Plaza ☎ 750-4400

France, 8. 934 Fifth Ave ☎ 606-3600

Germany, 40. 871 UN Pl ☎ 940-0400

Great Britain, 28. 845 Third Ave ☎ 745-0200

Greece, 4. 69 E 79th St ☎ 988-5500

Grenada, 71. 800 Second Ave ☎ 599-0301

Guatemala, 89. 57 Park Ave ☎ 686-3837

Guyana, 41. 866 UN Plaza ☎ 527-3215

Haiti, 85. 271 Madison Ave ☎ 697-9767

Honduras, 100. 80 Wall St ☎ 269-3611

Hungary, 30. 223 E. 52nd St ☎ 752-0669

Iceland, 46. 800 Third Ave ☎ 593-2700

India, 17. 3 E 64th St ☎ 774-0600

Indonesia, 13. 5 E 68th St ☎ 879-0600

Ireland, 49. 885 Second Ave ☎ 421-6934

Israel, 71. 800 Second Ave ☎ 499-5400

Italy, 12. 690 Park Ave ☎ 737-9100

Jamaica, 50. 767 Third Ave ☎ 935-9000

Japan, 55. 299 Park Ave ☎ 371-8222

Kuwait, 66. 321 E 44th St ☎ 973-4318

Lebanon, 6. 9 E 76th St ☎ 744-7905

Malaysia, 70. 313 E 43rd St ☎ 490-2722

Malta, 87. 249 E 35th St ☎ 725-2345

Mexico, 96. 27 E 39th St ☎ 217-6400

Morocco, 95. 10 E 40th St ☎ 758-2625

Myanmar, 5. 10 E 77th St ☎ 535-1310

Nepal, 22. 247 W. 87th St ☎ 874-2306

Netherlands, 35. 1 Rockefeller Plaza ☎ 246-1429

New Zealand, 48. 780 Third Ave ☎ 832-7420

Nicaragua, 69. 820 Second Ave ☎ 986-6562

Nigeria, 67. 828 Second Ave ☎ 850-2200

Norway, 42. 825 Third Ave ☎ 421-7333

Pakistan, 15. 12 E 65th St ☎ 879-5800

Paraguay, 76. 675 Third Ave ☎ 682-9441

Peru, 45. 241 E 49th St ☎ 646/735-3828

Airlines

Terminals

Airlines	JFK	LA GUARDIA	NEWARK
Aer Lingus ☎ 800/474-7424	4		
Aeroflot ☎ 888/340-6400	3		
Aerolineas Argentinas ☎ 800/333-0276	4		
Aeromar ☎ 877/237-6627	1		
AeroMexico ☎ 800/237-6639	3		
Air Canada ☎ 888/247-2262	7	CTB-A	A
Air France ☎ 800/237-2747	1		B
Air India ☎ 212/751-6200	4		
Air Jamaica ☎ 800/523-5585	2		B
Air Malta ☎ 800/756-2582	4		
Air Plus Comet ☎ 877/999-7587	4	CTB-C	
AirTran Airways ☎ 800/247-8726			A
Air Ukraine ☎ 212/230-1001	4		
Alaskan Airlines ☎ 800/426-0333			C
Alitalia ☎ 800/223-5730	1		B
All Nippon Airways ☎ 800/235-9262	3		
American ☎ 800/433-7300	8, 9	CTB-D	A
American Eagle ☎ 800/433-7300	9	CTB-C	
American Trans Air (ATA) ☎ 800/435-9282		CTB-C	B
America West ☎ 800/235-9292	7	CTB-B	A
Asiana Airlines ☎ 800/227-4262	4		
Austrian Airlines ☎ 800/843-0002	1		
Avianca ☎ 800/284-2622	3		
Biman Bangladesh ☎ 212/808-4477	4		
British Airways ☎ 800/247-9297	7		B
BWIA ☎ 800/538-2942	4		
Cathay Pacific ☎ 800/233-2742	7		
China Airlines ☎ 800/227-5118	3		
Colgan Air ☎ 800/428-4322		US Airways	
Continental ☎ 800/525-0280	4	CTB-A	A,C
Continental Connection ☎ 800/525-0280	4		
Continental Express ☎ 800/525-0280	4	CTB-A	C

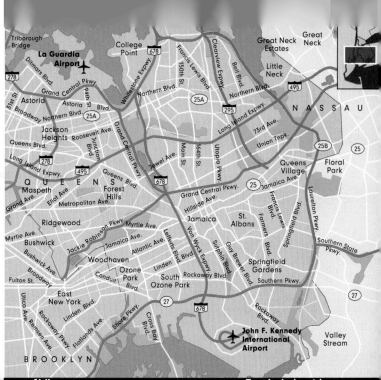

Airlines

	JFK	LA GUARDIA	NEWARK
Corsair ☎ 800/677-0720	4		
Czech Airlines ☎ 212/765-6545	3		
Delta ☎ 800/221-1212	3	Delta	B
Delta Connection ☎ 800/325-5205	3	Delta	
Delta Express ☎ 800/325-5205	2		B
Delta Shuttle ☎ 800/325-5205		MAT	
Egypt Air ☎ 800/334-6787	4		
El-Al ☎ 800/223-6700	4		B
Ethiopian ☎ 212/867-0095			B
EVA Airways ☎ 800/695-1188		CTB-C	B
Finnair ☎ 800/950-5000	8		
Frontier ☎ 800/432-1359			
Guyana ☎ 718/523-2300	4		
Iberia ☎ 800/772-4642	8		
Icelandair ☎ 800/223-5500	7		
Japan ☎ 800/525-3663	1		
JetBlue ☎ 800/538-2583	6		
KLM ☎ 800/374-7747	4		B
Korean ☎ 800/438-5000	1		
Kuwait ☎ 800/458-9248	4		
Lacsa Airlines ☎ 800/225-2272	2		
Lan Chile ☎ 800/735-5526	4		
Lan Peru ☎ 800/735-5590	4		
LOT Polish ☎ 800/223-0593	8		B
Lufthansa ☎ 800/645-3880	1		B
Malaysia ☎ 800/582-9264			B
Malev Hungarian ☎ 800/223-6884	3		
Mexicana ☎ 800/531-7921		CTB-B	B
Midway ☎ 800/446-4392		CTB-D	
Midwest Express ☎ 800/452-2022			B
National ☎ 888/757-5387	4		A
Nigeria Airways ☎ 212/972-4565	4		

Terminals (cont.)

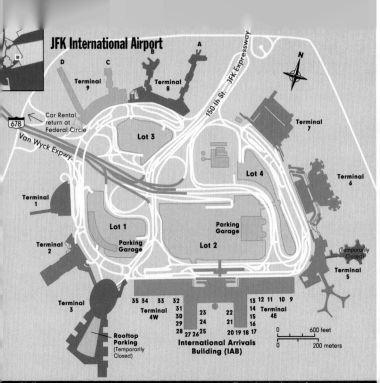

JFK International Airport

Terminal 9
Terminal 8
Terminal 7
Terminal 6
Terminal 5 *(Temporarily Closed)*
Terminal 1
Terminal 2
Terminal 3
Terminal 4W
Terminal 4E

Car Rental return at Federal Circle

Van Wyck Expwy.
JFK Expressway
150 th St.
678

Lot 3
Lot 4
Lot 1
Lot 2

Parking Garage
Parking Garage

Rooftop Parking *(Temporarily Closed)*

35 34 33 32 31 30 29 28 27 26 25 24 23 22 21 20 19 18 17 16 15 14 13 12 11 10 9

International Arrivals Building (IAB)

0   600 feet
0   200 meters

Airlines

	JFK	LA GUARDIA	NEWARK
North American ☎ 718/656-2650	4		B
Northwest ☎ 800/225-2525	4	Delta	B
Olympic ☎ 800/223-1226	1		
Pakistan ☎ 212/370-9157	4		
Qantas ☎ 800/227-4500	7		A
Royal Air Maroc ☎ 800/344-6726	1		
Royal Jordanian ☎ 212/949-0050	3		
Sabena ☎ 800/955-2000	4		B
SAS ☎ 800/221-2350			B
Saudi Arabian ☎ 800/472-8342	2		
Shuttle America ☎ 888/999-3273		CTB-B	
Singapore Airlines ☎ 800/742-3333	1		B
South African Airways ☎ 800/722-9675	3		
Spirit ☎ 800/772-7117		CTB-C	A
Tarom-Romanian ☎ 212/560-0840	4		
TACA International ☎ 800/535-8780	2		
TAP Air Portugal ☎ 800/221-7370	4		B
Turkish Airlines ☎ 800/874-8875	1		
United ☎ 800/241-6522	7	CTB-C	A
United Express ☎ 800/241-6522	7	CTB-C	A
Universal ☎ 718/441-4900	T4		A
US Airways ☎ 800/428-4322		US Airways	A
US Airways Express ☎ 800/428-4322		US Airways	A
US Airways Shuttle ☎ 800/428-4322		US Airways Shuttle	
Uzbekistan Airways ☎ 212/245-1005	4		
Vanguard ☎ 800/826-4827		CTB-B	
Varig ☎ 800/468-2744	4		
Virgin Atlantic ☎ 800/862-8621	1		B
World Airways ☎ 770/632-8000	4		

Terminals (cont.)

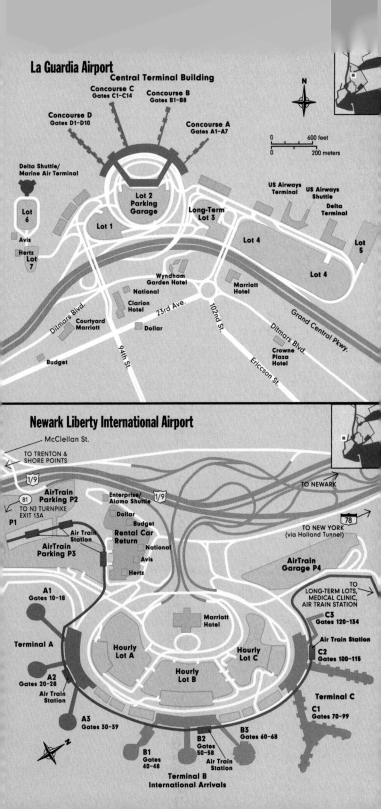

La Guardia Airport

Central Terminal Building

Concourse C
Gates C1–C14

Concourse B
Gates B1–B8

Concourse D
Gates D1–D10

Concourse A
Gates A1–A7

N

0   600 feet
0   200 meters

Delta Shuttle/
Marine Air Terminal

Lot 2
Parking
Garage

Long-Term
Lot 3

Lot 1

US Airways
Terminal

US Airways
Shuttle

Delta
Terminal

Lot 6

Lot 4

Avis

Hertz
Lot 7

Lot 4

Lot 5

Wyndham
Garden Hotel

Marriott
Hotel

National

Clarion
Hotel

23rd Ave.

102nd St.

Ditmars Blvd.

Courtyard
Marriott

Dollar

Grand Central Pkwy.

94th St.

Ditmars Blvd

Crowne
Plaza
Hotel

Ericsson St.

Budget

Newark Liberty International Airport

McClellan St.

TO TRENTON &
SHORE POINTS

1/9

TO NEWARK

AirTrain
Parking P2

Enterprise/
Alamo Shuttle

1/9

81

TO NJ TURNPIKE
EXIT 13A

P1

Dollar

Budget

78

TO NEW YORK
(via Holland Tunnel)

Air Train
Station

Rental Car
Return

AirTrain
Parking P3

National

AirTrain
Garage P4

Avis

Hertz

TO
LONG-TERM LOTS,
MEDICAL CLINIC,
AIR TRAIN STATION

A1
Gates 10–18

Marriott
Hotel

C3
Gates 120–134

Terminal A

Hourly
Lot A

Hourly
Lot C

Air Train Station

C2
Gates 100–115

A2
Gates 20–28

Hourly
Lot B

Air Train
Station

Terminal C

A3
Gates 30–39

C1
Gates 70–99

B3
Gates 60–68

B2
Gates
50–58

B1
Gates
40–48

Air Train
Station

Terminal B
International Arrivals

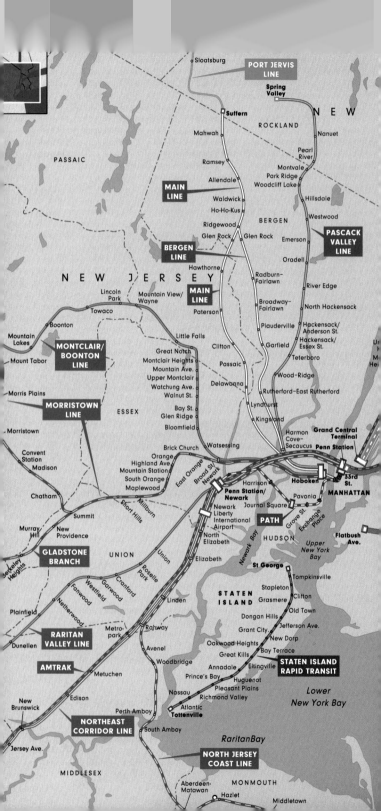

NEW YORK

Ossining
Chappaqua
New Canaan
Scarborough
Pleasantville
Talmadge Hill
Springdale
Hawthorne
Mount Pleasant
Glenbrook
Rowa.
Philipse Manor
Valhalla
Darien
AMTRAK
HUDSON LINE
Noroton Heights
Tarrytown
Stamford
Irvington
North White Plains
CONNECTICUT
Ardsley
White Plains
HARLEM LINE
Cos Cob
Riverside
Old Greenwich
Dobbs Ferry
Hartsdale
AMTRAK
Hastings
Greenwich
Scarsdale
Port Chester
WESTCHESTER
Crestwood
Rye
Greystone
Tuckahoe
Harrison
Glenwood
Bronxville
Mamaroneck
Long Island Sound
OYSTER BAY BRANCH
Fleetwood
Mt. Vernon
Mount Vernon W.
Fairfield?

Hudson River

Yonkers
Pelham
Larchmont
Ludlow
NEW HAVEN LINE
Locust Valley
Glen Cove
Cold Spring Harbor
Riverdale
Wakefield
New Rochelle
Glen Street
Oyster Bay
Spuyten Duyvil
Woodlawn
Sea Cliff
PORT JEFFERSON BRANCH
Marble Hill
Williams Bridge
Glen Head
University Heights
Botanical Garden
PORT WASHINGTON BRANCH
Greenvale
Syosset
Morris Heights
Fordham
Port Washington
NASSAU
Tremont
AMTRAK
Plandome
Roslyn
BRONX
Melrose
Great Neck
Albertson
Hicksville
Bethpage
East River
Manhasset
East Williston
Westbury
125th St.
La Guardia Airport
Plandome
Minneola
Carle Place
Hunterspoint Ave.
New Hyde Park
Nassau Blvd.
Country Life Press
RONKONKOMA BRANCH
Woodside
Little Neck
Merillon Ave.
Garden City
Massapequa
Broadway
Douglaston
Stewart Manor
Auburndale
Murray Hill
Bayside
Nassau Blvd.
Hempstead
Shea Stadium
Flushing Main St.
Floral Park
Bellmore
QUEENS
Forest Hills
Kew Gdns.
Jamaica
Bellerose
West Hempstead
Merrick
Hollis
Queens Village
Henpstead Gdns.
Nostrand Ave.
St. Albans
Lakeview
Rockville Centre
Seaford
East New York
Locust Manor
Malverne
Baldwin
Wantagh
BROOKLYN
Kennedy International Airport
Laurelton
Westwood
Centre Ave.
Freeport
Rosedale
Valley Stream
Gibson
Lynbrook
Hewlett
East Rockaway
Oceanside
Inwood
Woodmere
Cedarhurst
Island Park
Far Rockaway
Lawrence
Long Beach
BABYLON BRANCH/ MONTAUK BRANCH

ATLANTIC OCEAN

N

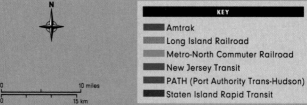

KEY
Amtrak
Long Island Railroad
Metro-North Commuter Railroad
New Jersey Transit
PATH (Port Authority Trans-Hudson)
Staten Island Rapid Transit

0   10 miles
0   15 km

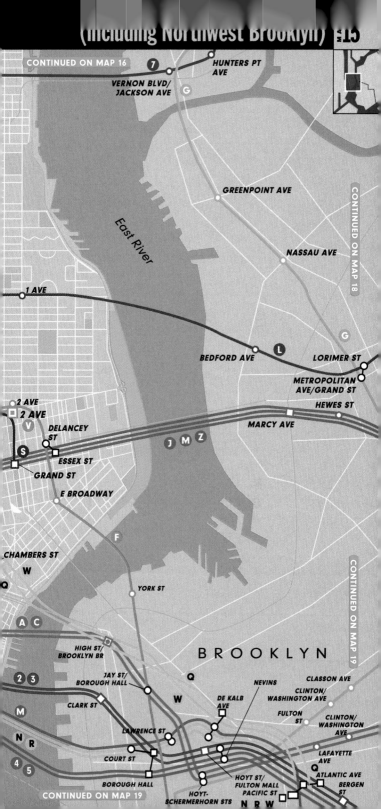

CONTINUED ON MAP 16

7
HUNTERS PT
AVE

VERNON BLVD/
JACKSON AVE

G

GREENPOINT
AVE

East River

NASSAU AVE

CONTINUED ON MAP 18

1 AVE

G

BEDFORD AVE

L

LORIMER ST

METROPOLITAN
AVE/GRAND ST

HEWES ST

2 AVE
2 AVE
V

DELANCEY
ST

MARCY AVE

J M Z

S

ESSEX ST

GRAND ST

E BROADWAY

F

CHAMBERS ST
W

Q

YORK ST

CONTINUED ON MAP 19

A C

BROOKLYN

HIGH ST/
BROOKLYN BR

2 3

JAY ST/
BOROUGH HALL

Q

CLASSON AVE

CLINTON/
WASHINGTON AVE

W

DE KALB
AVE

NEVINS

M

CLARK ST

FULTON
ST

CLINTON/
WASHINGTON
AVE

N R

LAWRENCE ST

4 5

COURT ST

LAFAYETTE
AVE

Q

ATLANTIC AVE

BERGEN
ST

BOROUGH HALL

HOYT ST/
FULTON MALL
PACIFIC ST

HOYT-
SCHERMERHORN STS

N R W

CONTINUED ON MAP 19

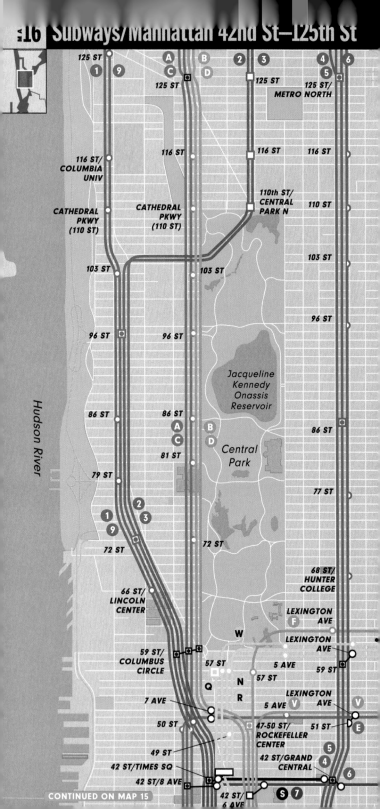

125 ST ① ⑨
Ⓐ Ⓑ ② ③ ④ ⑥
Ⓒ Ⓓ
125 ST
125 ST
125 ST/
METRO NORTH

116 ST/
COLUMBIA
UNIV
116 ST
116 ST
116 ST

CATHEDRAL
PKWY
(110 ST)
CATHEDRAL
PKWY
(110 ST)
110th ST/
CENTRAL
PARK N
110 ST

103 ST
103 ST
103 ST

96 ST
96 ST
96 ST

*Jacqueline
Kennedy
Onassis
Reservoir*

86 ST
86 ST
Ⓐ Ⓑ
86 ST
Ⓒ Ⓓ
81 ST

*Central
Park*

79 ST

77 ST

② ③
① ⑨
72 ST
72 ST

68 ST/
HUNTER
COLLEGE

66 ST/
LINCOLN
CENTER

LEXINGTON
Ⓕ AVE

Ⓦ
LEXINGTON
AVE

59 ST/
COLUMBUS
CIRCLE
57 ST
5 AVE
59 ST

Ⓠ Ⓝ
57 ST
Ⓡ
LEXINGTON
AVE

7 AVE
5 AVE Ⓥ Ⓥ

50 ST
51 ST
Ⓔ

47-50 ST/
ROCKEFELLER
CENTER

49 ST
⑤
42 ST/GRAND
CENTRAL
④

42 ST/TIMES SQ
42 ST/8 AVE
⑥

42 ST/
6 AVE
Ⓢ ⑦

Hudson River

CONTINUED ON MAP 15

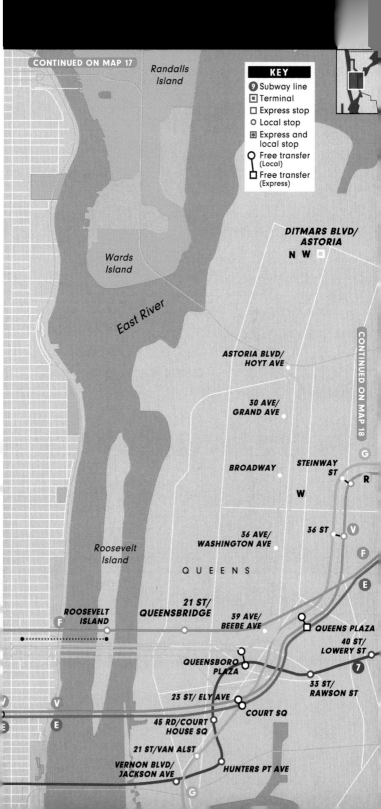

CONTINUED ON MAP 17

Randalls
Island

KEY
- **9** Subway line
- ◨ Terminal
- ☐ Express stop
- ○ Local stop
- ◉ Express and local stop
- ⬭ Free transfer (Local)
- ⬮ Free transfer (Express)

Wards
Island

East River

DITMARS BLVD/ ASTORIA
N W ☐

CONTINUED ON MAP 18

ASTORIA BLVD/ HOYT AVE

30 AVE/ GRAND AVE

BROADWAY

STEINWAY ST
W

G

R

36 AVE/ WASHINGTON AVE

36 ST
V

F

E

Roosevelt
Island

Q U E E N S

21 ST/ QUEENSBRIDGE

ROOSEVELT ISLAND
F

39 AVE/ BEEBE AVE

QUEENS PLAZA

40 ST/ LOWERY ST

QUEENSBORO PLAZA

33 ST/ RAWSON ST

7

23 ST/ ELY AVE

COURT SQ

V

E

45 RD/ COURT HOUSE SQ

21 ST/VAN ALST

VERNON BLVD/ JACKSON AVE

HUNTERS PT AVE

G

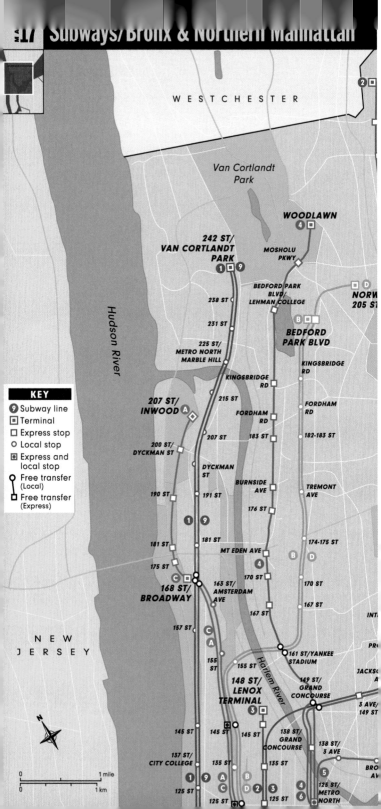

W E S T C H E S T E R

Van Cortlandt Park

WOODLAWN
4

MOSHOLU PKWY

242 ST/
VAN CORTLANDT
PARK
1 9

238 ST

BEDFORD PARK
BLVD/
LEHMAN COLLEGE

NORW
205 ST

231 ST

D

225 ST/
METRO NORTH
MARBLE HILL

B

BEDFORD
PARK BLVD

207 ST/
INWOOD
A

KINGSBRIDGE
RD

KINGSBRIDGE
RD

215 ST

Hudson River

FORDHAM
RD

FORDHAM
RD

200 ST/
DYCKMAN ST

207 ST

183 ST

182-183 ST

DYCKMAN
ST

190 ST

191 ST

BURNSIDE
AVE

TREMONT
AVE

176 ST

1 9

181 ST

181 ST

174-175 ST

175 ST

MT EDEN AVE

B

D

C

4

168 ST/
BROADWAY

170 ST

163 ST/
AMSTERDAM
AVE

170 ST

167 ST

167 ST

157 ST

C

C

A

161 ST/YANKEE
STADIUM

INT

PR

N E W
J E R S E Y

155
ST

155 ST

Harlem River

JACKS
A

148 ST/
LENOX
TERMINAL

149 ST/
GRAND
CONCOURSE

3 AVE/
149 ST

3

145 ST

145 ST

145 ST

138 ST/
GRAND
CONCOURSE

138 ST/
3 AVE

137 ST/
CITY COLLEGE

135 ST

135 ST

135 ST

5

BRO
AV

1 9

A

B

4

125 ST/
METRO
NORTH

C

D

2

3

125 ST

6

125 ST

125 ST

KEY

9 Subway line
☐ Terminal
☐ Express stop
○ Local stop
☐ Express and local stop
○ Free transfer (Local)
☐ Free transfer (Express)

N

0   1 mile
0   1 km

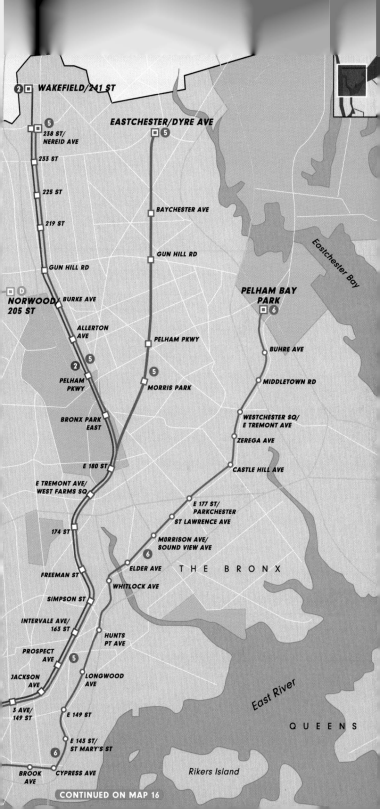

2 WAKEFIELD/241 ST

EASTCHESTER/DYRE AVE

5 238 ST/
NEREID AVE

233 ST

225 ST

219 ST

BAYCHESTER AVE

GUN HILL RD

GUN HILL RD

D
NORWOOD
205 ST

BURKE AVE

PELHAM BAY
PARK **6**

ALLERTON
AVE

PELHAM PKWY

BUHRE AVE

2 **5**

PELHAM
PKWY

5
MORRIS PARK

MIDDLETOWN RD

BRONX PARK
EAST

WESTCHESTER SQ/
E TREMONT AVE

ZEREGA AVE

E 180 ST

CASTLE HILL AVE

E TREMONT AVE/
WEST FARMS SQ

E 177 ST/
PARKCHESTER
ST LAWRENCE AVE

174 ST

MORRISON AVE/
SOUND VIEW AVE

6

FREEMAN ST

ELDER AVE

T H E   B R O N X

WHITLOCK AVE

SIMPSON ST

INTERVALE AVE/
163 ST

HUNTS
PT AVE

PROSPECT
AVE

JACKSON
AVE

5

LONGWOOD
AVE

East River

3 AVE/
149 ST

E 149 ST

Q U E E N S

6

E 145 ST/
ST MARY'S ST

BROOK
AVE

CYPRESS AVE

Rikers Island

Eastchester Bay

CONTINUED ON MAP 16

KEY
- **9** Subway line
- ◧ Terminal
- ◻ Express stop
- ○ Local stop
- ◎ Express and local stop
- ○ Free transfer (Local)
- ☐ Free transfer (Express)

✈ LaGuardia Airport

DITMARS BLVD/ ASTORIA N W

WILLETS POINT/ SHEA STADIUM

111 ST

103 ST/CORONA PLAZA

JUNCTION BLVD

90 ST/ELMHURST AVE

ASTORIA BLVD/ HOYT AVE

30 AVE/ GRAND AVE W

BROADWAY

STEINWAY ST

46 ST V **NORTHERN BLVD**

65 ST

74 ST/ BROADWAY

82 ST/ JACKSON HTS V

ELMHURST AVE

GRAND AVE/ NEWTOWN

WOODHAVEN BLVD/ QUEENS MALL

36 AVE 36 ST

36 ST

69 ST/ FISK AVE

ROOSEVELT AVE/ JACKSON HTS

39 AVE G R

61 ST/ WOODSIDE

E F R G

63 DRIVE/ REGO PARK

7 **52 ST**

QUEENS PLAZA

46 ST/ BLISS ST

40 ST/ LOWERY ST

33 ST/ RAWSON ST

QUEENSBORO PLAZA

Q U E E N S

MIDDLE VILLAGE/ METROPOLITAN AVE M

FRESH POND RD

FOREST AVE

G

GREENPOINT AVE

SENECA AVE

NASSAU AVE

GRAHAM AVE

JEFFERSON ST

DEKALB AVE

MYRTLE AVE

HALSEY ST

L **BEDFORD AVE**

LORIMER ST

GRAND ST

MORGAN AVE

WYCKOFF AVE

METROPOLITAN AVE/GRAND ST

MONTROSE AVE

KNICKERBOCKER

WILSON AVE

J M **HEWES ST**

BROADWAY LORIMER ST

M **CENTRAL AVE**

BUSHWICK AVE/ ABERDEEN ST

MARCY AVE

FLUSHING AVE

Z **MYRTLE AVE**

KOSCIUSKO ST

GATES AVE

HALSEY ST

BROADWAY/ EASTERN PKWY

FLUSHING AVE

CHAUNCEY ST

ROCKAWAY AVE

BROADWAY/ EAST NEW YORK ATLANTIC AVE

MYRTLE/ WILLOUGHBY

B R O O K L Y N

A C

SUTTER AVE

BEDFORD/NOSTRAND

RALPH AVE

CLASSON AVE

KINGSTON AVE/ THROOP AVE

NOSTRAND AVE

UTICA AVE

ROCKAWAY AVE

G

FRANKLIN AVE

SARATOGA AVE

FULTON

CLINTON/ WASHINGTON AVE S

SUTTER AVE/ RUTLAND RD

CONTINUED ON MAP 16
CONTINUED ON MAP 15
CONTINUED ON MAP 19

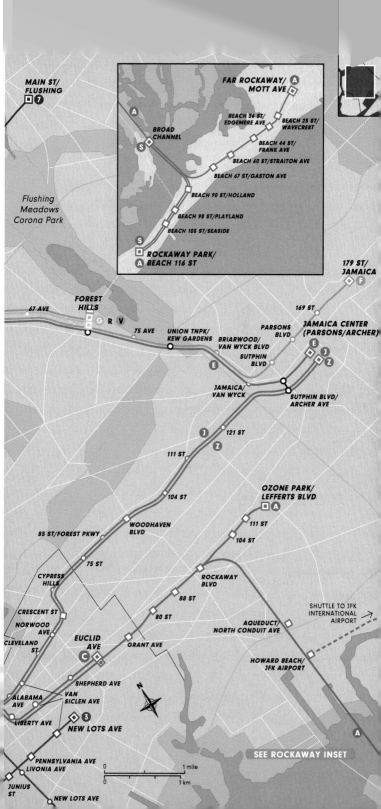

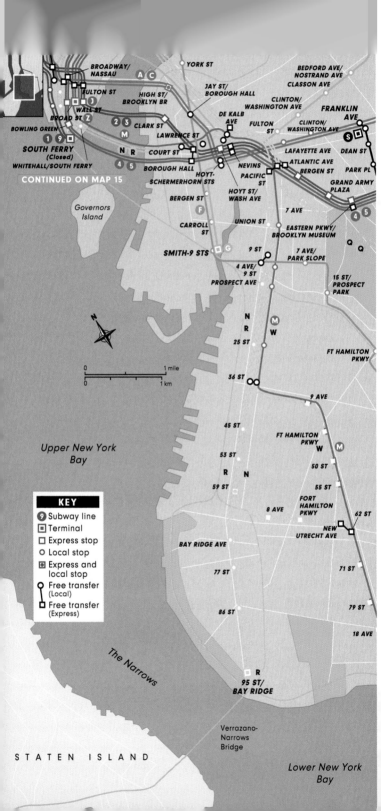

BROADWAY/
NASSAU

YORK ST

BEDFORD AVE/
NOSTRAND AVE
CLASSON AVE

FULTON ST

HIGH ST/
BROOKLYN BR

JAY ST/
BOROUGH HALL

CLINTON/
WASHINGTON AVE

FRANKLIN
AVE

WALL ST

BROAD ST

DE KALB
AVE

CLINTON/
WASHINGTON AVE

BOWLING GREEN

CLARK ST

LAWRENCE ST

FULTON
ST

SOUTH FERRY
WHITEHALL/SOUTH FERRY

COURT ST

LAFAYETTE AVE

DEAN ST

PARK PL

(Closed)

BOROUGH HALL

ATLANTIC AVE
BERGEN ST

HOYT-
SCHERMERHORN STS

NEVINS
PACIFIC
ST

GRAND ARMY
PLAZA

CONTINUED ON MAP 15

BERGEN ST

HOYT ST/
WASH AVE

7 AVE

Governors
Island

CARROLL
ST

UNION ST

EASTERN PKWY/
BROOKLYN MUSEUM

SMITH-9 STS

9 ST

7 AVE/
PARK SLOPE

4 AVE/
9 ST
PROSPECT AVE

15 ST/
PROSPECT
PARK

N
R

25 ST

M
W

FT HAMILTON
PKWY

36 ST

9 AVE

Upper New York
Bay

45 ST

FT HAMILTON
PKWY
W

53 ST

50 ST

R
N
59 ST

55 ST

8 AVE

FORT
HAMILTON
PKWY

62 ST

NEW
UTRECHT
AVE

KEY

Subway line

Terminal

Express stop

Local stop

Express and
local stop

Free transfer
(Local)

Free transfer
(Express)

BAY RIDGE AVE

77 ST

71 ST

86 ST

79 ST

18 AVE

The Narrows

95 ST/
BAY RIDGE

R

STATEN ISLAND

Verrazano-
Narrows
Bridge

Lower New York
Bay

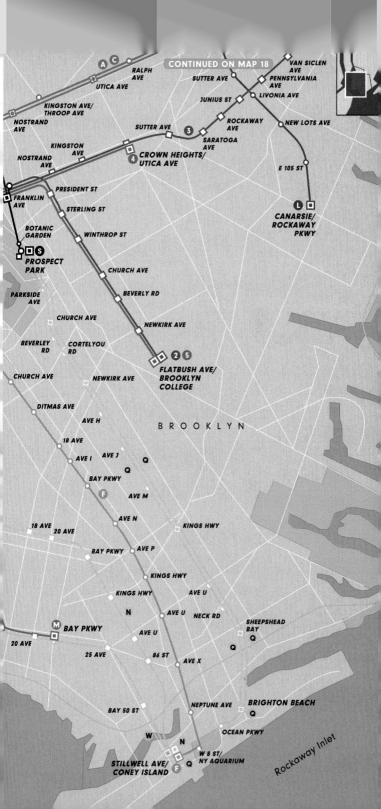

CONTINUED ON MAP 18

Ⓐ Ⓒ

RALPH
AVE

VAN SICLEN
AVE

SUTTER AVE

PENNSYLVANIA
AVE

UTICA AVE

LIVONIA AVE

JUNIUS ST

KINGSTON AVE/
THROOP AVE

ROCKAWAY
AVE

NEW LOTS AVE

NOSTRAND
AVE

SUTTER AVE

❸

SARATOGA
AVE

KINGSTON
AVE

❹

CROWN HEIGHTS/
UTICA AVE

E 105 ST

NOSTRAND
AVE

PRESIDENT ST

Ⓛ

FRANKLIN
AVE

STERLING ST

CANARSIE/
ROCKAWAY
PKWY

BOTANIC
GARDEN

WINTHROP ST

Ⓢ

PROSPECT
PARK

CHURCH AVE

PARKSIDE
AVE

BEVERLY RD

CHURCH AVE

NEWKIRK AVE

BEVERLEY
RD

CORTELYOU
RD

CHURCH AVE

NEWKIRK AVE

❷ ❺

FLATBUSH AVE/
BROOKLYN
COLLEGE

DITMAS AVE

B R O O K L Y N

AVE H

18 AVE

AVE J

AVE I

Q

BAY PKWY

Q

Ⓕ

AVE M

AVE N

18 AVE

20 AVE

KINGS HWY

BAY PKWY

AVE P

KINGS HWY

AVE U

KINGS HWY

AVE U

AVE U

NECK RD

SHEEPSHEAD
BAY

N

Ⓜ

BAY PKWY

AVE U

Q

20 AVE

25 AVE

86 ST

Q

AVE X

BAY 50 ST

NEPTUNE AVE

BRIGHTON BEACH

Q

W

OCEAN PKWY

N

Ⓦ

Ⓝ Ⓠ

STILLWELL AVE/
CONEY ISLAND

Ⓕ

W 8 ST/
NY AQUARIUM

Rockaway Inlet

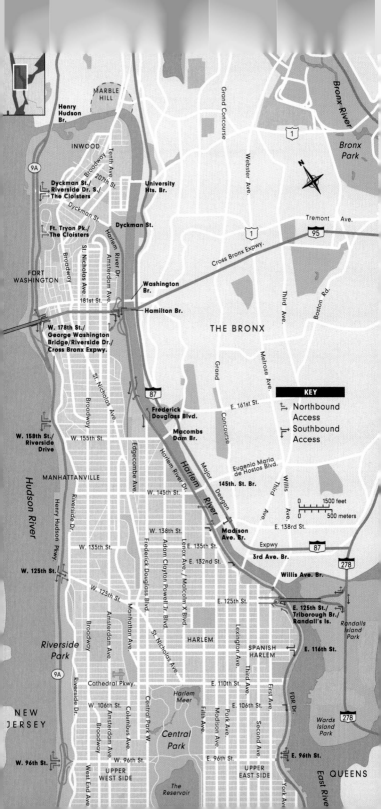

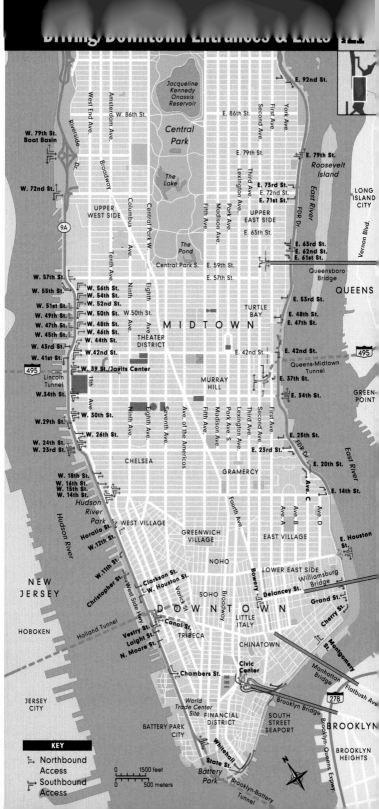

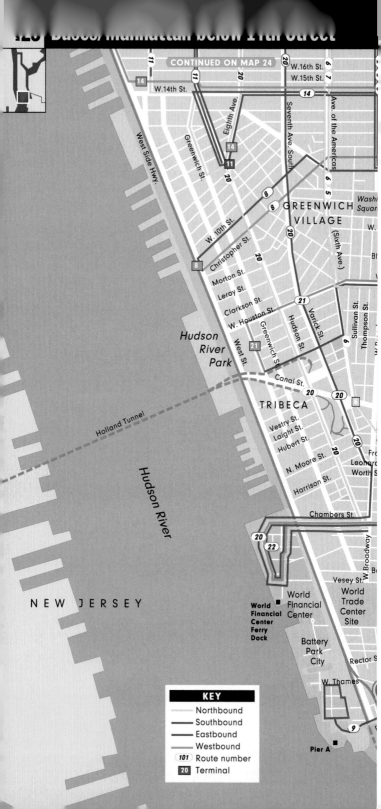

CONTINUED ON MAP 24

W.16th St.
W.15th St.
W.14th St.

Eighth Ave.

Greenwich St.

West Side Hwy.

Seventh Ave. South

Ave. of the Americas

GREENWICH
VILLAGE

Washi
Squar

W.

(Sixth Ave.)

W. 10th St.

Christopher St.

Morton St.

Leroy St.

Clarkson St.

W. Houston St.

Greenwich St.

Sullivan St.

Thompson St.

Hudson
River
Park

West St.

Varick St.

Hudson St.

Canal St.

TRIBECA

Holland Tunnel

Vestry St.

Laight St.

Hubert St.

N. Moore St.

Harrison St.

Fra
Leonard
Worth S

Hudson River

Chambers St.

NEW JERSEY

World
Financial
Center
Ferry
Dock

World
Financial
Center

W. Broadway

Vesey St.

World
Trade
Center
Site

W. Be

Battery
Park
City

Rector S

W. Thames

Pier A

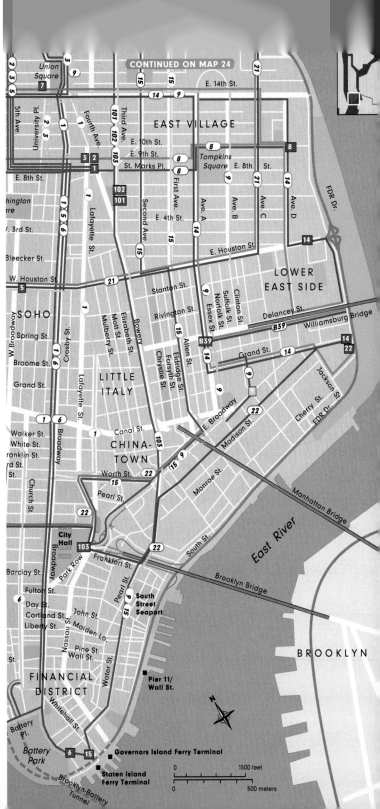

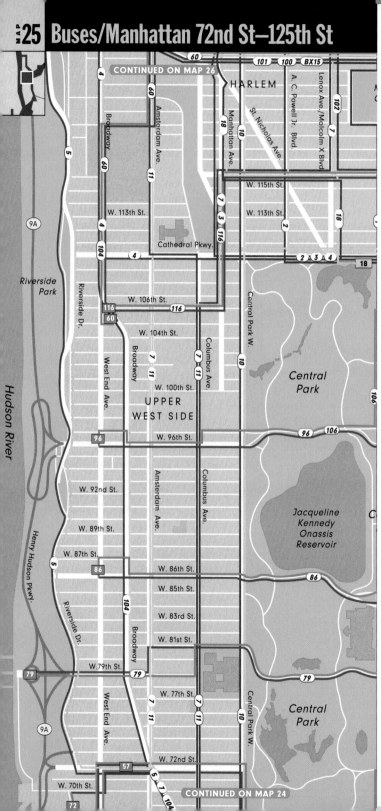

MAP 25 **Buses/Manhattan 72nd St–125th St**

CONTINUED ON MAP 26

HARLEM

Broadway

Amsterdam Ave.

St. Nicholas Ave.

Manhattan Ave.

A. C. Powell Jr. Blvd.

Lenox Ave./Malcolm X Blvd.

W. 115th St.

W. 113th St.

W. 113th St.

Cathedral Pkwy.

Central Park W.

W. 106th St.

W. 104th St.

W. 100th St.

Columbus Ave.

UPPER WEST SIDE

Riverside Park

Riverside Dr.

West End Ave.

Broadway

W. 96th St.

Central Park

W. 92nd St.

W. 89th St.

W. 87th St.

Amsterdam Ave.

Columbus Ave.

Jacqueline Kennedy Onassis Reservoir

Hudson River

W. 86th St.

W. 85th St.

W. 83rd St.

Riverside Dr.

Broadway

W. 81st St.

Henry Hudson Pkwy.

W. 79th St.

W. 77th St.

Central Park W.

Central Park

W. 72nd St.

West End Ave.

W. 70th St.

CONTINUED ON MAP 24

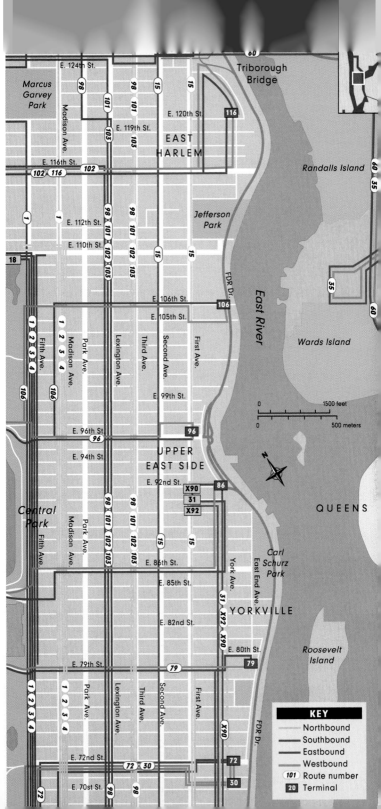

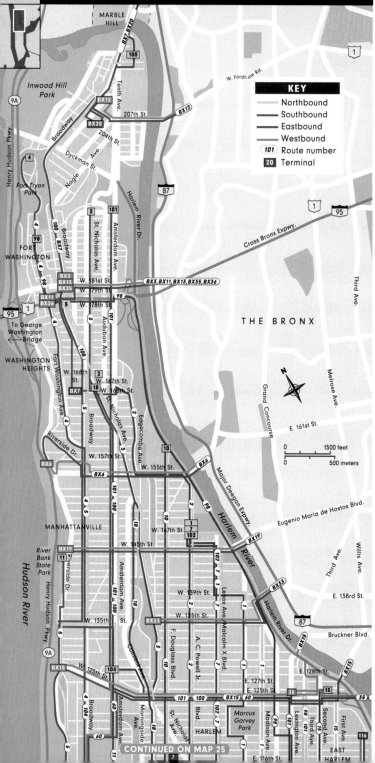

CONTINUED ON MAP 25

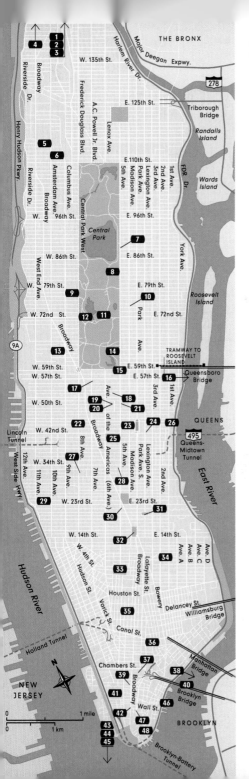

Listed Alphabetically

Bartow-Pell Mansion, 1.
895 Shore Rd N, Pelham Bay Park,
Bronx ☎ 718/885-1461

Bayard Building, 34.
65-69 Bleecker St

Belvedere Castle, 10. Vista Rock, at
the base of Central Park's Great Lawn

Brooklyn Bridge, 43. City Hall Park to
Cadman Plaza, over East River

Carnegie Hall, 14.
Seventh Ave & 57th St
☎ 247-7800

Castle Clinton, 47.
Battery Park ☎ 344-7220

**Charlton-King-Vandam Historic
District, 35.** between Houston and
Vandam Sts

Chrysler Building, 22.
Lexington Ave & 42nd St

City Hall/City Hall Park, 40.
Broadway, south of Chambers St
☎ 788-6865

The Cloisters, 3. Fort Tryon Park
☎ 923-3700

Colonnade Row, 30. Lafayette St,
between E 4th St & Astor Pl

Daily News Building, 15.
220 E 42nd St

The Dakota, 11.
W 72nd St & Central Park West

Eldridge Street Synagogue, 37.
12 Eldridge St ☎ 978-8800

Empire State Building, 26.
Fifth Ave & 34th St ☎ 736-3100

Federal Hall National Memorial, 44.
28 Wall St ☎ 825-6888

Flatiron Building, 28.
Fifth Ave & 23rd St

Fraunces Tavern, 46.
Broad & Pearl Sts ☎ 425-1778

Grace Church, 31.
Broadway & 10th St ☎ 254-2000

Grand Central Terminal, 21.
Park Ave, between 42nd & 44th Sts

Guggenheim Museum, 6.
1071 Fifth Ave ☎ 423-3600

Haughwout Building, 38.
488 Broadway

Henderson Place Historic District, 7.
York Ave & 86th St

Lever House, 16. 390 Park Ave

Lincoln Center, 12.
Broadway between 62nd & 66th
Sts
☎ 875-5350

Merchant's House, 34.
29 E 4th St ☎ 777-1089

MetLife Building, 20.
1 Madison Ave

Metropolitan Museum of Art, 8.
Fifth Ave & 82nd St ☎ 535-7710

Morris Jumel Mansion, 4.
160th St & Jumel Ter ☎ 923-8008

Municipal Building, 39.
Centre & Chambers Sts

National Arts Club, 29.
15 Gramercy Park S

**New York Life Insurance Company
Building, 27.** Madison Ave & 26th St

New York Public Library, 24.
Fifth Ave, between 40th & 42nd Sts
☎ 930-0800

New York Stock Exchange, 45.
8 Broad St ☎ 656-5165

Pierpont Morgan Library, 25.
29 E 36th St ☎ 685-0008

The Plaza Hotel, 13.
Fifth Ave & 59th St

Rockefeller Center, 18.
Fifth Ave & 50th St

St. John the Divine, 5.
Amsterdam Ave & 112th St ☎ 316-7540

St. Paul's Chapel, 42.
Broadway & Fulton St ☎ 602-0874

Seagram Building, 17. 375 Park Ave
☎ 572-7404

Singer Building, 36. 561 Broadway

UN Headquarters, 23.
First Ave, between 42nd & 48th Sts
☎ 963-7713

Van Cortlandt House, 2.
Broadway & 246th St, Bronx
☎ 718/543-3344

Villard Houses, 19.
451-455 Madison Ave

Washington Mews, 32.
between Fifth Ave & Univ Pl

Whitney Museum, 9.
Madison Ave & 75th St ☎ 570-3676

Woolworth Building, 41.
233 Broadway

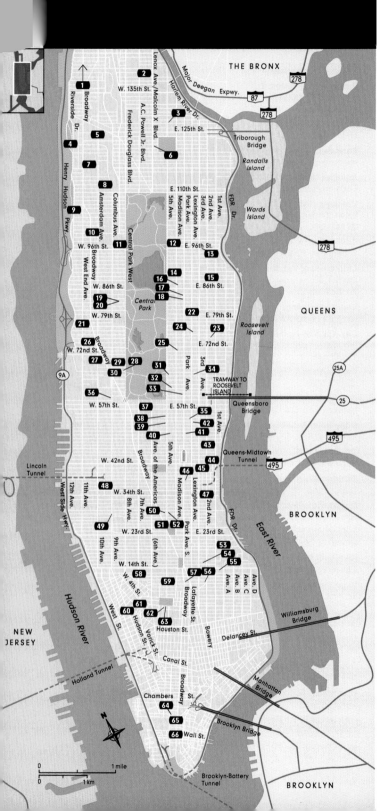

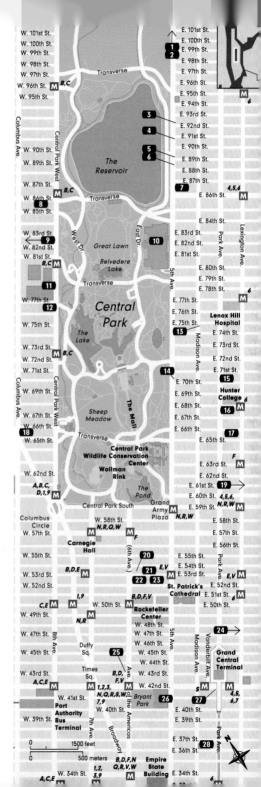

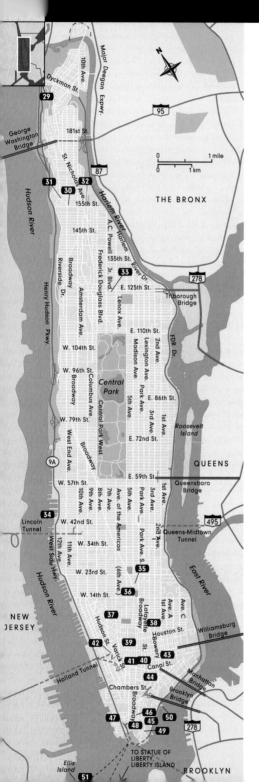

Listed Alphabetically

American Craft Museum, 22.
40 W 53rd St ☎ 956-3535

American Folk Art Museum, 20.
45 W 53rd St ☎ 265-1040

American Folk Art Museum, Feld Gallery, 18. 2 Lincoln Sq ☎ 595-9533

American Mus of Natural History/ Rose Ctr for Earth & Space, 11.
Central Park W & 79th St ☎ 769-5100

American Numismatic Society, 30.
Broadway & 155th St ☎ 234-3130

The Americas Society, 16.
680 Park Ave ☎ 249-8950

Asia Society Gallery, 15.
725 Park Ave ☎ 288-6400

Bard Graduate Center for Decorative Arts and Design, 8.
18 W 86th St ☎ 501-3000

Children's Museum of Manhattan, 9.
212 W 83rd St ☎ 721-1234

Children's Museum of the Arts, 40.
182 Lafayette St ☎ 274-0986

China Institute Gallery, 17.
125 E 65th St ☎ 744-8181

The Cloisters, 29. Fort Tryon Park
☎ 923-3700

Cooper-Hewitt National Design, 4.
2 E 91st St ☎ 860-8400

Ellis Island Immigration, 51.
Ellis Island ☎ 363-3200

Forbes Magazine Galleries, 37.
62 Fifth Ave ☎ 206-5548

Fraunces Tavern, 49.
54 Pearl St ☎ 425-1778

Frick Collection, 14. 1 E 70th St
☎ 288-0700

Guggenheim, 6. 1071 Fifth Ave
☎ 423-3500

Hispanic Society of America, 31.
Broadway & W 155th St ☎ 926-2234

International Ctr of Photography, 25.
1133 Sixth Ave ☎ 860-1777

Intrepid Sea-Air-Space, 34. Pier 86,
Twelfth Ave & W 46th St ☎ 245-0072

Japan Society, 24. 333 E 47th St
☎ 832-1155

Jewish Museum, 3. 1109 Fifth Ave
☎ 423-3200

Lower East Side Tenement Museum, 43. 90 Orchard St ☎ 431-0233

Merchant's House, 38.
29 E 4th St ☎ 777-1089

Metropolitan Museum of Art, 10.
1000 Fifth Ave ☎ 535-7710

Morgan Library, 28.
29 E 36th St ☎ 685-0008

Morris-Jumel Mansion, 32.
65 Jumel Ter ☎ 923-8008

Mount Vernon Hotel, 19. 421 E 61st St
☎ 838-6878

El Museo del Barrio, 1. 1230 Fifth Ave
☎ 831-7272

Museum for African Art, 39.
593 Broadway ☎ 966-1313

Museum of American Financial History, 46. 28 Broadway ☎ 908-4519

Museum of the American Indian, 48.
1 Bowling Green ☎ 514-3700

Museum of Chinese in the Americas, 44. 70 Mulberry St ☎ 619-4785

Museum of the City of NY, 2.
1220 Fifth Ave ☎ 534-1672

Museum of Jewish Heritage, 47.
18 First Place ☎ 968-1800

Museum of Modern Art (MoMA), 21.
11 W 53rd St ☎ 708-9400 (closed through
Spring 2005, see Queens listings)

Museum of Television & Radio, 23.
25 W 52nd St ☎ 621-6600

National Academy of Design, 5.
1083 Fifth Ave ☎ 369-4880

Neue Galerie, 7. 1048 Fifth Ave
☎ 628-6200

New Museum of Contemporary Art, 41. 583 Broadway ☎ 219-1222

NYC Fire Museum, 42. 278 Spring St
☎ 691-1303

NY Historical Society, 12.
170 Central Park W ☎ 873-3400

NY Public Library, 26.
Fifth Ave & 42nd St ☎ 869-8089

Police Museum, 45. 100 Old Slip
☎ 480-3100

South Street Seaport, 50. Pier 17,
Fulton & South Sts ☎ 732-8257

Studio Museum in Harlem, 33.
144 W 125th St ☎ 864-4500

Theodore Roosevelt Birthplace, 35.
28 E 20th St ☎ 260-1616

Whitney Museum at Philip Morris, 27.
120 Park Ave ☎ 917/663-2453

Whitney Museum of American Art, 13.
945 Madison Ave ☎ 570-3676

Yeshiva University Museum, 36.
15 W 16th St ☎ 294-8330

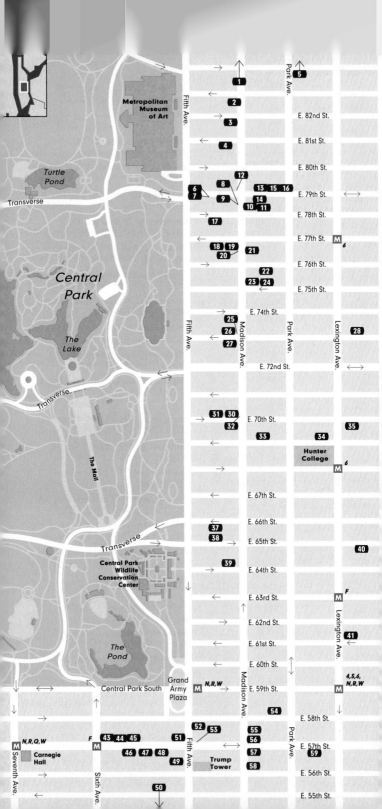

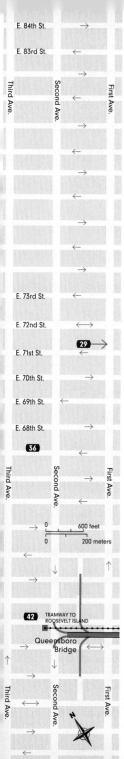

Listed by Site Number

Mary Ryan, 47. 24 W 57th St
☎ 397-0669

McKee, 52. 745 Fifth Ave ☎ 688-5951

Michael Rosenfeld, 47. 24 W 57th St
☎ 247-0082

Michael Werner, 18. 4 E 77th St
☎ 988-1623

Mitchell-Innes & Nash, 9.
1018 Madison Ave ☎ 744-7400

Nohra Haime, 58. 595 Madison Ave
☎ 888-3550

O'Hara, 56. 41 E 57th St ☎ 355-3330

Owen, 24. 19 E 75th St ☎ 879-2415

Pace MacGill, 57. 32 E 57th St
☎ 759-7999

Pace Wildenstein, 57. 32 E 57th St
☎ 421-3292

Paul McCarron, 8. 1014 Madison Ave
☎ 772-1181

Peter Findlay, 56. 41 E 57th St
☎ 644-4433

Reece, 47. 24 W 57th St ☎ 333-5830

Richard Gray, 9. 1018 Madison Ave
☎ 472-8787

Richard York, 38. 21 E 65th St
☎ 772-9155

Ronin, 55. 605 Madison Ave
☎ 688-0188

Ruth Horowitz, 35. 160A E 70th St
☎ 717-9067

Safani, 20. 980 Madison Ave
☎ 570-6360

Salander-O'Reilly, 7. 20 E 79th St
☎ 879-6606

Schlesinger, 27. 24 E 73rd St
☎ 734-3600

Schmidt Bingham, 56. 41 E 57th St
☎ 888-1122

Shepherd + Derom, 14. 58 E 79th St
☎ 861-4050

Skarskedt, 9. 1018 Madison Ave
☎ 737-2060

Solomon & Co, 23. 959 Madison Ave
☎ 737-8200

Sotheby's, 29. 1334 York Ave
☎ 606-7000

Soufer, 10. 1015 Madison Ave
☎ 628-3225

Spanierman, 54. 45 E 58th St
☎ 832-0208

Steltman, 56. 41 E 57th St
☎ 317-9200

Susan Sheehan, 48.
20 W 57th St ☎ 489-3331

Throckmorton, 41. 153 E 61st St
☎ 223-1059

Tibor de Nagy, 49. 724 Fifth Ave
☎ 262-5050

Ubu, 17. 16 E 78th St ☎ 794-4444

The Uptown, 1. 1194 Madison Ave
☎ 722-3677

Wally Findlay, 59. 124 E 57th St
☎ 421-5390

Wildenstein, 39. 19 E 64th St
☎ 879-0500

Zabriskie, 56. 41 E 57th St
☎ 752-1223

Zwirner & Wirth, 33. 32 E 69th St
☎ 517-8677

W. 26th St.
W. 26th St.
W. 25th St.
W. 25th St.

CHELSEA

W. 24th St.
W. 24th St.

W. 23rd St.
W. 23rd St.

W. 22nd St.
W. 22nd St.

W. 21st St.
W. 21st St.

W. 20th St.
W. 20th St.
W. 19th St.
W. 19th St.

Eleventh Ave.
Tenth Ave.
Twelfth Ave.

Art Galleries/SoHo

New York University
Houston St.

F, S
M
5

SOHO

Sullivan St.
Thompson St.
Wooster St.
Greene St.
Mercer St.
Broadway
Crosby St.
W. Broadway
MacDougal St.

Prince St.
Prince St.

N, R
M

C, E

Spring St.

Ave. of the Americas
(Sixth Ave.)

Sullivan St.
Thompson St.
Mercer St.
Broadway
Crosby St.

Broome St.
Broome St.

0   300 feet
0   100 meters

N

Grand St.
Grand St.

Chelsea Galleries
Listed Alphabetically

AC Project Room, 30.
453 W 17th St ☎ 645–4970

ACA, 34. 529 W 20th St ☎ 206–8080

Andrea Rosen, 15. 525 W 24th St
☎ 627–6000

Barbara Gladstone, 17.
515 W 24th St ☎ 206–9300

Caren Golden, 2. 526 W 26th St
☎ 727–8304

Cheim & Reid, 3. 547 W 25th St
☎ 242–7727

Clementine, 7. 526 W 26th St
☎ 243–5937

D'Amelio Terras, 21. 525 W 22nd St
☎ 352–9460

Dia Center for the Arts, 27.
548 W 22nd St ☎ 989–5566

Fischbach, 11. 210 Eleventh Ave
☎ 759–2345

Fredericks-Freiser, 24. 504 W 22nd St
☎ 633–6555

Gagosian, 12. 555 W 24th St
☎ 741–1111

Galerie Lelong, 6. 528 W 26th St
☎ 315–0470

Greene Naftali, 7. 526 W 26th St
☎ 463–7770

Henry Urbach Architecture, 7.
526 W 26th St ☎ 627–0974

Holly Solomon, 25. 222 W 23rd St
☎ 941–5777

Klotz-Sirmon, 9. 511 W 25th St
☎ 741–4764

Lehmann Maupin, 5. 540 W 26th St
☎ 965–0753

Luhring Augustine, 14. 531 W 24th St
☎ 206–9100

Mary Boone, 13. 541 W 24th St
☎ 752–2929

Matthew Marks, 23. 522 W 22nd St
☎ 243–1650

Max Protech, 22. 511 W 22nd St
☎ 633–6999

Maynes, 34. 529 W 20th St
☎ 741–3318

Metro Pictures, 16. 519 W 24th St
☎ 206–7100

Paula Cooper, 32. 534 W 21st St
☎ 255–1105

Postmasters, 31. 459 W 19th St
☎ 727–3323

Ricco/Maresca, 34. 529 W 20th St
☎ 627–4819

Robert Mann, 11. 210 11th Ave
☎ 989–7600

Robert Miller, 8. 524 W 26th St
☎ 366–4774

Sandra Gering, 29. 534 W 22nd St
☎ 646/336–7183

Sarah Morthland, 18. 225 Tenth Ave
☎ 242–7767

Sepia, 19. 148 W 24th St ☎ 645–9444

Shainman, 33. 513 W 20th St
☎ 645–1701

Sonnabend, 28. 536 W 22nd St
☎ 627–1018

Stark, 2. 555 W 25th St ☎ 807–1051

Team, 1. 527 W 26th St ☎ 279–9219

303, 21. 525 W 22nd St ☎ 255–1121

Van de Weghe, 20. 521 W 23rd St
☎ 929–6633

Viridian Artists, 4. 530 W 25th St
☎ 414–4040

Wessel + O'Connor, 10.
242 W 26th St ☎ 242–8811

Yancey Richardson, 26.
535 W 22nd St ☎ 343–1255

Soho Galleries
Listed Alphabetically

American Primitive, 6.
594 Broadway ☎ 966–1530

Ariel Meyerowitz, 9. 580 Broadway
☎ 625–3434

Art in General, 39. 79 Walker St
☎ 219–0473

Artists Space, 37. 38 Greene St
☎ 226–3970

Atlantic, 34. 40 Wooster St
☎ 219–3183

Bridgewater/Lustberg & Blumenfeld, 12. 560 Broadway
☎ 941–6355

Brooke Alexander, 29.
59 Wooster St ☎ 925–4338

Bruce R Lewin, 15. 136 Prince St
☎ 431–4750

Cavin-Morris, 12. 560 Broadway
☎ 226–3768

Ceres, 8. 584–588 Broadway
☎ 226–4725

Curt Marcus, 10. 578 Broadway
☎ 226-3200

David Zwirner, 35. 43 Greene St
☎ 966-9074

Deitch Projects, 36. 76 Grand St
☎ 343-7300

Deitch Projects, 43. 18 Wooster St
☎ 343-7300

Dia Center for the Arts, 27.
393 W Broadway ☎ 989-5566

Dia Center for the Arts, 14.
141 Wooster St ☎ 989-5566

Dieu Donné Papermill, 31.
433 Broome St ☎ 226-0573

The Drawing Center, 33.
35 Wooster St ☎ 219-2166

Exit Art, 22. 548 Broadway
☎ 966-7745

55 Mercer, 38. 55 Mercer St
☎ 226-8513

Gallery 292, 20. 120 Wooster St
☎ 431-0292

Grant, 41. 7 Mercer St ☎ 343-2919

Grey, 1. 100 Washington Sq E
☎ 998-6780

Howard Greenberg, 20.
120 Wooster St ☎ 334-0010

John Gibson, 11. 568 Broadway
☎ 925-1192

June Kelly, 7. 591 Broadway
☎ 226-1660

Leica, 5. 670 Broadway ☎ 777-3051

Lennon Weinberg, 12. 560 Broadway
☎ 941-0012

Luise Ross, 11. 568 Broadway
☎ 343-2161

Margarete Roeder, 23.
545 Broadway ☎ 925-6098

Meisel, 18. 141 Prince St ☎ 677-1340

Michael Ingbar, 11. 568 Broadway
☎ 334-1100

Mimi Ferzt, 13. 114 Prince St
☎ 343-9377

Nancy Hoffman, 19.
429 W Broadway ☎ 966-6676

Nolan/Eckman, 12. 560 Broadway
☎ 925-6190

OK Harris, 28. 383 W Broadway
☎ 431-3600

Pace Wildenstein, 3.
142 Greene St ☎ 431-9224

Peter Blum, 24. 99 Wooster St
☎ 343-0441

Phoenix, 11. 568 Broadway
☎ 226-8711

Phyllis Kind, 4. 136 Greene St
☎ 925-1200

PPOW, 30. 476 Broome St
☎ 941-8642

Ruesch, 26. 134 Spring St ☎ 925-1137

Ronald Feldman, 42. 31 Mercer St
☎ 226-3232

Sally Hawkins, 16. 448 W Broadway
☎ 477-5699

SoHo Triad, 40. 107 Grand St
☎ 965-9500

SoHo 20, 23. 545 Broadway
☎ 226-4167

Sperone Westwater, 3.
142 Greene St ☎ 431-3685

Sragow, 25. 73 Spring St ☎ 219-1793

Staley-Wise, 12. 560 Broadway
☎ 966-6223

Stephen Haller, 12. 560 Broadway
☎ 219-2500

Susan Teller, 11. 568 Broadway
☎ 941-7335

Swiss Institute, 32. 495 Broadway
☎ 925-2035

Tony Shafrazi, 21. 119 Wooster St
☎ 274-9300

Vorpal, 2. 459 W Broadway
☎ 777-3939

Ward-Nasse, 17. 178 Prince St
☎ 925-6951

Westwood, 10. 578 Broadway
☎ 925-5700

Woodward, 35. 476 Broome St
☎ 966-3411

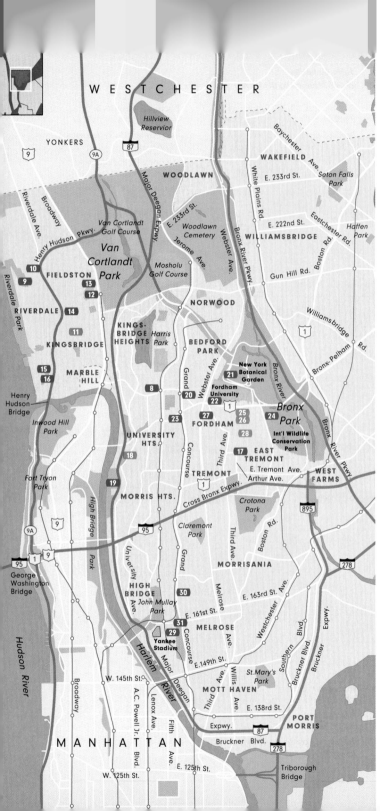

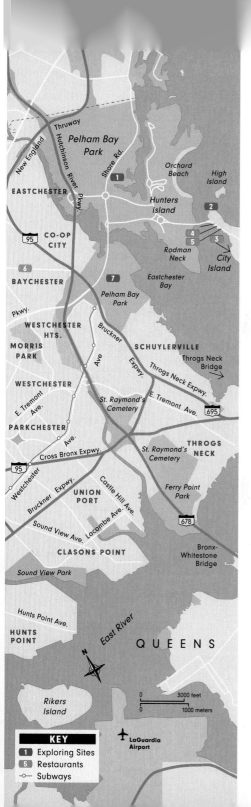

KEY
1 Exploring Sites
5 Restaurants
○— Subways

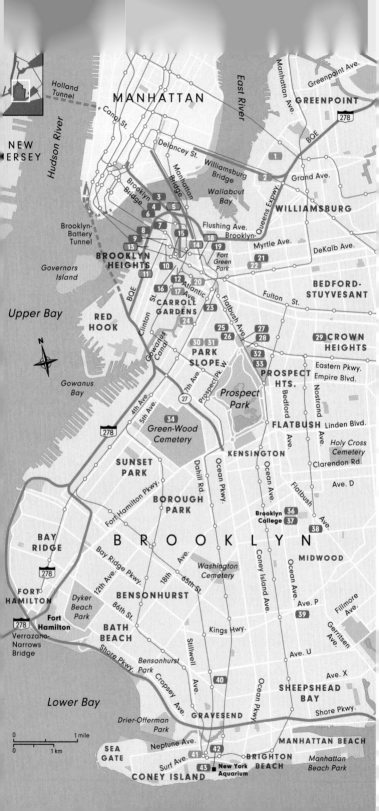

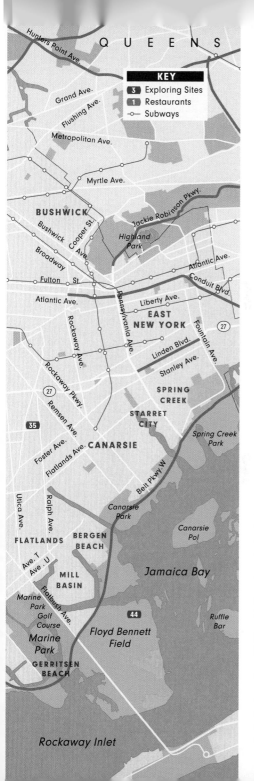

KEY

3 Exploring Sites
1 Restaurants
—○— Subways

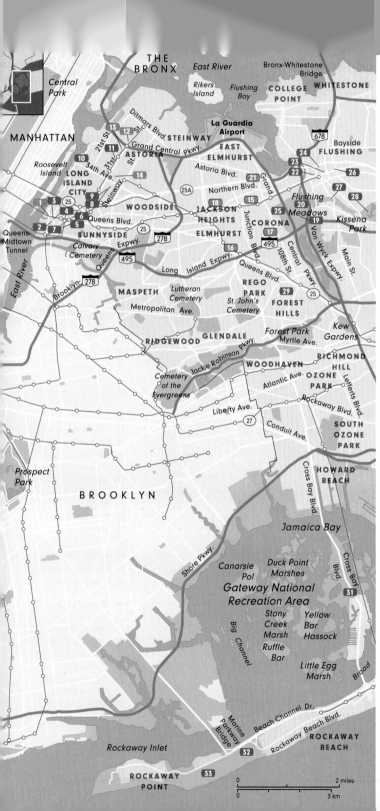

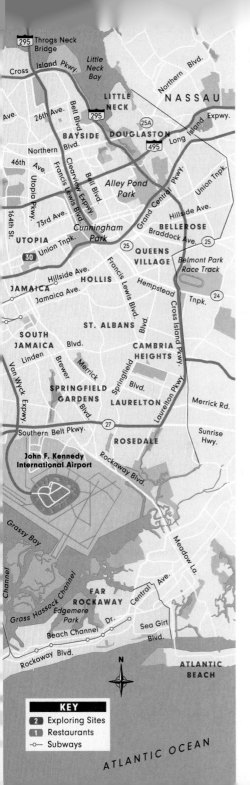

NEW JERSEY

Newark Bay

Kill Van Kull

ST. GEORGE

The Narrows

② ①

③ NEW BRIGHTON

Castleton Ave.

Bayonne Bridge

Terr.

Bay St.

STAPLETON

PORT IVORY

Richmond

PORT RICHMOND

⑥

ROSEBANK

Goethals Bridge

Forest Ave.

④

⑤

⑦ ⑧

95

278

WESTERLEIGH

Victory Blvd.

278

Verrazano-Narrows Bridge

BLOOMFIELD

Staten Island Expwy.

GRASMERE

SOUTH BEACH

BULLS HEAD

CHELSEA

GRANT CITY

440

RICHMONDTOWN

DONGAN HILLS

NEW DORP BEACH

West Shore Expwy.

La Tourette Park

⑨

Richmond Rd.

⑩

Arthur Kill

Arthur Kill

Richmond Rd.

Giffords La.

Amboy Rd.

Hylan Blvd.

OAKWOOD

Gateway National Recreation Area

⑪

ROSSVILLE

Arden Ave.

ELTINGVILLE

⑬ ⑫

Great Kills Harbor

Woodrow Ave.

Huguenot Ave.

ANNADALE

Ave.

⑭

N

ATLANTIC OCEAN

WOODROW

440

Richmond Pkwy.

Ave.

Outerbridge Crossing

440

STATEN ISLAND RAPID TRANSIT

PRINCES BAY

0   2 miles

0   3 km

Hylan Blvd.

TOTTENVILLE

Raritan Bay

KEY

① Exploring Sites

⑤ Restaurants

○ Staten Island Rapid Transit

Outer Boroughs Listed Alphabetically

BRONX SITES

Arthur Ave Italian Market, 17.
Arthur Ave, betw E Fordham Rd &
E Tremont Ave

Bartow-Pell Mansion, 1.
895 Shore Rd N & Pelham Bay Pkwy
☎ 718/885-1461

Bronx County Courthouse, 31.
851 Grand Concourse ☎ 718/590-3640

Bronx Museum of the Arts, 30.
1040 Grand Concourse ☎ 718/681-6000

Bronx Zoo (IWCP), 24. Fordham Rd &
Southern Blvd ☎ 718/367-1010

Christ Church, 10. Henry Hudson Pkwy
& 252nd St

City Island, 2. Long Island Sound

Creston Ave Baptist Church, 23.
114 E 188th St ☎ 718/367-1754

Edgar Allan Poe Cottage, 20.
Grand Concourse & E Kingsbridge Rd
☎ 718/881-8900

Edgehill Church, 16.
2550 Independence Ave ☎ 718/549-7324

**Enrico Fermi Cultural Center/Library,
27.** 610 E 186th St ☎ 718/933-6410

Fordham University, 22.
441 E Fordham Rd ☎ 718/817-1000

Henry Hudson Memorial, 15.
Independence Ave & W 227th St

Kingsbridge Armory, 8.
Kingsbridge Rd & Jerome Ave

Manhattan College, 13.
Manhattan College Pkwy & W 242nd St
☎ 718/862-8000

NY Botanical Garden, 21. Southern
Blvd & 200th St ☎ 718/817-8700

Pelham Bay Park, 7. Pelham Bay

Roberto Clemente State Park, 19.
W Tremont Ave & Matthewson Rd
☎ 718/299-8750

**Van Cortlandt House Museum,
12.** B'way & W 246th St
☎ 718/543-3344

Wave Hill, 9. 249th St &
Independence Ave ☎ 718/549-3200

World War I Memorial Tower, 14.
Riverdale Ave & 239th St

BRONX RESTAURANTS

Ann & Tony's Restaurant, 25.
2407 Arthur Ave ☎ 718/933-1469.
Italian. $$-$$$$

Bellavista Cafe, 11. 554 W 235th St
☎ 718/933-1469. Italian. $$

Dominick's, 26. 2335 Arthur Ave
☎ 718/733-2807. Italian. $-$$$

Il Boschetto Finest Italian, 6.
1660 E Gun Hill Rd ☎ 718/379-9335.
Italian. $$

Jimmy's Bronx Cafe, 18.
281 W Fordham Rd ☎ 718/329-2000.
Pan-Latin. $-$$$

King Lobster, 5. 500 City Island Ave
☎ 718/885-1579. Seafood. $$-$$$

Le Refuge Inn, 4. 620 City Island Ave
☎ 718/885-2478. French. $$$-$$$$

Press Café, 29. 114 E 157th St
☎ 718/401-0545. Italian. $

Roberto's, 28. 632 E 186th St
☎ 718/733-9503. Italian. $$-$$$

Sammy's Fish Box, 3. 41 City Island
Ave ☎ 718/885-0920. Seafood. $-$$

BROOKLYN SITES

Bargemusic, Ltd, 6. Fulton Ferry
Landing, Old Fulton St & Waterfront
☎ 718/624-4061

Bklyn Acad of Music (BAM), 23.
30 Lafayette Ave ☎ 718/636-4100

Bklyn Borough Hall, 15.
209 Joralemon St

Bklyn Botanic Garden, 33. 900
Washington Ave ☎ 718/623-7200

Bklyn Bridge, 3. Cadman Plaza,
Bklyn, to City Hall Park, Manhattan

**Bklyn Center of Performing Arts,
37.** Brooklyn College, Campus Rd
☎ 718/951-4500

Bklyn Children's Museum, 29.
145 Brooklyn Ave ☎ 718/735-4400

Bklyn College CUNY, 36. 2900
Bedford Ave ☎ 718/951-5000

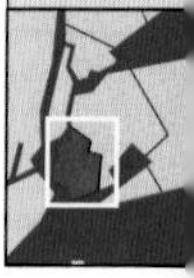

MAP **34**

BROOKLYN SITES (cont.)

Bklyn Conservatory of Music, 25.
58 7th Ave ☎ 718/622-3300

Brooklyn Historical Society, 9.
128 Pierrepont St ☎ 718/222-4111

Brooklyn Museum of Art, 32.
200 Eastern Pkwy ☎ 718/638-5000

Brooklyn Public Library, 28.
Grand Army Plaza ☎ 718/230-2100

Church of St Ann & the Holy Trinity, 10.
157 Montague St

Coe House, 38. 1128 E 34th St

Coney Island Amusement Park, 43.
Surf Ave ☎ 718/372-0275

Fulton Ferry Pier, 4. Foot of Old Fulton St

Gateway National Recreation Area, 44. Floyd Bennett Field, Flatbush Ave & Shore Pkwy ☎ 718/338-3799

Green-Wood Cemetery, 34.
Fifth Ave & 25th St ☎ 718/768-7300

Long Island Univ, 19. Univ Plaza, DeKalb & Flatbush Aves
☎ 718/488-1000

Montauk Club, 26. 25 Eighth Ave
☎ 718/638-0800

NY Aquarium, 42. Boardwalk & W 8th St
☎ 718/265-FISH

NY Transit Museum, 16. Boerum Pl & Schermerhorn St ☎ 718/694-5100

Old Gravesend Cemetery, 40.
Gravesend Neck Rd & MacDonald Ave

Plymouth Church, 7. 75 Hicks St
☎ 718/624-4743

Pratt Institute, 21. 200 Willoughby Ave
☎ 718/636-3600

The Promenade, 8. Between
Montague & Clark Sts

Soldiers' & Sailors' Memorial Arch, 27.
Flatbush Ave & Eastern Pkwy

State St Houses, 12. 290-324 State St

Wyckoff House/Pieter Claesen, 35.
5816 Clarendon Rd ☎ 718/629-5400

Wyckoff-Bennett Homestead, 39.
1669 E 22nd St

BROOKLYN RESTAURANTS

Brooklyn Blue Ribbon, 30. 280 Fifth
Ave ☎ 718/840-0404. American. $$

Caffe Buon Gusto, 12. 151 Montague
St ☎ 718/624-3838. Italian. $$

Cucina, 31. 256 Fifth Avenue
☎ 718/230-0711. Italian. $$-$$$

Gage & Tollner, 13. 372 Fulton St
☎ 718/875-5181. American. $$$

Gargiulo's Restaurant, 39. 2911
W 15th St ☎ 718/266-4891. Italian. $$

Henry's End, 10. 44 Henry St
☎ 718/834-1776. New American. $$

Junior's Restaurant, 16. 386 Flatbush
Ave ☎ 718/852-5257. American. $

Madiba, 22. 195-197 DeKalb Ave
☎ 718/855-9190. South African. $-$$

Monte's, 22. 451 Carroll St
☎ 718/624-8984. Italian. $$

Moustache, 19. 405 Atlantic Ave
☎ 718/852-5555. Middle Eastern. $

Oznot's Dish, 1. 79 Berry St
☎ 718/599-6596. Middle Eastern. $-$$

Peter Luger Steak House, 2. 178 B'way
☎ 718/387-7400. Steak. $$$

River Cafe, 4. 1 Water St
☎ 718/522-5200. New American. $$$$

Saul, 17. 140 Smith St ☎ 718/935-9844.
New American. $$

MAP 35

QUEENS SITES

American Museum of the Moving Image, 9. 35th Ave & 36th St ☎ 718/784-0077

Bowne House, 23.
37-01 Bowne St ☎ 718/359-0528

Court House Square, 4.
45th Ave & 21st St

Flushing Meadows-Corona Park, 20. College Point Blvd & Grand Central Pkwy ☎ 718/760-6565

Fort Tilden, 33. Breezy Pt
☎ 718/318-4300

Friends Meeting House, 24.
137-16 Northern Blvd ☎ 718/358-9636

Hunter's Point Historic District, 5.
45th Ave & 21st-23rd Sts

Isamu Noguchi Garden Museum, 10.
32-37 Vernon Blvd ☎ 718/204-7088
(closed through 2004; call for
temporary location)

Jacob Riis Park, 33. Marine Bridge
Pkwy at Rockaway Pt Blvd
☎ 718/318-4300

Jamaica Bay Wildlife Refuge, 31.
Broad Channel & First Rd
☎ 718/318-4300

Kaufman Astoria Studios, 8.
34-12 36th St ☎ 718/392-5600

Kissena Park, 28.
Rose Ave & Parsons Blvd

QUEENS SITES (cont.)

MoMA QNS, 6. 45-20 33rd St
☎ 718/708-9400

NY Hall of Science, 25. 47-01 111th St
☎ 718/699-0005

PS 1 Contemporary Art Center, 2.
22-25 Jackson Ave ☎ 718/784-2084

Queens Botanical Gardens, 27.
43-50 Main St ☎ 718/886-3800

Queens Historical Society, 22.
143-35 37th Ave ☎ 718/939-0647

Queens Museum of Art, 19. Flushing
Meadows-Corona Park ☎ 718/592-5555

Silvercup Studios, 3. 42-25 21st St
☎ 718/784-3390

St Demitrios, 11. 30-11 30th Dr
☎ 718/728-1718

St John's University, 30.
8000 Utopia Pkwy ☎ 718/990-6161

Weeping Beech Tree, 26.
37th Ave & Parsons Blvd

West Side Tennis Club, 29.
1 Tennis Pl ☎ 718/268-2300

QUEENS RESTAURANTS

Bohemian Hall and Park, 14.
21-19 24th Ave
☎ 718/728-9776. Czech. $

Elias Corner, 12. 31st St & 24th Ave
☎ 718/932-1510. Seafood. $$

Green Field, 21. 108-01 Northern Blvd
☎ 718/672-5202. Brazilian. $$

Jackson Diner, 18. 37-47 74th St
☎ 718/672-1232. Indian. $

Jai-Ya Thai, 16. 81-11 Broadway
☎ 718/651-1330. Thai. $

Manducatis, 7. 13-27 Jackson Ave
☎ 718/729-4602. Italian. $-$$

Park Side, 17. 107-01 Corona Ave
☎ 718/271-9276. Italian. $$

Piccola Venezia, 13. 42-01 28th Ave
☎ 718/721-8470. Italian. $$-$$$

Tierras Columbianas, 15.
82-18 Roosevelt Ave ☎ 718/426-8868.
Colombian. $

Water's Edge Restaurant, 1.
44th Dr at East River ☎ 718/482-0033.
American. $$$-$$$$

STATEN ISLAND SITES

Alice Austin House Museum, 8.
2 Hylan Blvd ☎ 718/816-4506

Garibaldi-Meucci Museum, 7.
420 Tompkins Ave ☎ 718/442-1608

**Gateway National Recreation
Area, 11.** Fort Wadsworth
☎ 718/354-4500

**Historic Richmondtown/Staten
Island Historical Society, 10.**
441 Clarke Ave ☎ 718/351-1611

**Jacques Marchais Museum of
Tibetan Art, 9.** 338 Lighthouse Ave
☎ 718/987-3500

Museum of Staten Island, 2.
75 Stuyvesant Pl ☎ 718/727-1135

Snug Harbor Cultural Center, 3.
1000 Richmond Ter ☎ 718/448-2500

Staten Island Botanical Garden, 3.
1000 Richmond Terrace
☎ 718/273-8200

Staten Island Ferry, 1.
St George Station, Richmond Terrace
& Hyatt St ☎ 718/815-2628

Staten Island Institute, 2.
75 Stuyvesant Pl ☎ 718/727-1135

Staten Island Zoo, 4.
614 Broadway ☎ 718/442-3100

MAP 36

STATEN ISLAND RESTAURANTS

Aesop's Tables, 6. 1233 Bay St
☎ 718/720-2005. New American.
$$-$$$

Angelina's, 14. 26 Jefferson Blvd
☎ 718/227-7100. Italian. $$$

Arirang, 13. 23A Nelson Ave
☎ 718/966-9600. Japanese/Steak.
$$-$$$

Denino's Pizzeria, 5.
524 Port Richmond Ave
☎ 718/442-9401. Pizza. $

Marina Cafe, 12. 154 Mansion Ave
☎ 718/967-3077. American. $$$

$$$$ = *over $32* $$$ = *$25-$32* $$ = *$15-$24* $ = *under $15*
Based on cost per person for an entrée.

KEY

- ■ Playing Fields
- ■ Vest-Pocket Parks
- ≋ Swimming Pools
- ◎ Tennis Courts
- ⚘ Horse Stables

MARBLE HILL

Kingsbridge Rd.

Grand Concourse

Bronx River

Baker Field

Inwood Hill Park

9A

INWOOD

Isham Park

207th St.

Tenth Ave.

UNIVERSITY HTS

Bronx Park

Broadway

Dyckman St.

Nagle Ave.

Highbridge Park

Harlem

River Dr.

Amsterdam Ave.

TREMONT

Tremont Ave.

Fort Tryon park

Fort Washington Park

WASHINGTON HEIGHTS

St. Nicholas Ave.

MORRIS HTS

1

95

W. 181st St.

Cross Bronx Expwy.

Claremont Park

Crotona Park

Third Ave.

Boston Rd.

95

1

George Washington Bridge

J. Hood Wright Park

Audubon Ave.

University Ave.

MORRISANIA

Fort Washington Ave.

Broadway

St. Nicholas Ave.

Highbridge Park

87

HIGH BRIDGE

John Mullaly Park

Macombs Dam Park

THE BRONX

Melrose Ave.

E. 163rd St.

Westchester Ave.

E. 161st St.

MELROSE

Grand Concourse

0   1500 feet
0   500 meters

Franz Sigel Park

Eugenio Maria de Hostos Blvd.

St. Mary's Park

Southern Blvd.

Bruckner Blvd.

W. 155th St.

Trinity Cemetery

Fort Washington Park

Jackie Robinson Park

Edgecombe Ave.

Major Deegan

Harlem River

Willis Ave.

Third Ave.

Hudson River

Henry Hudson Pkwy.

Riverbank State Park

Amsterdam Ave.

Convent Ave.

W. 145th St.

Colonel Young Park

MOTT HAVEN

E. 138th St.

PORT MORRIS

Sakura Park

St. Nicholas Park

W. 135th St.

Frederick Douglass Blvd.

Adam Clayton Powell Jr. Blvd.

Lenox Ave. / Malcolm X Blvd.

Harlem River Dr.

Expwy.

Bruckner Blvd.

87

278

Riverside Dr.

Sheltering Arms Park

W. 138th St.

Harlem River Drive Park

Randalls Island Park

W. 125th St.

MORNINGSIDE HEIGHTS

Manhattan Ave.

Morningside Ave.

St. Nicholas Ave.

Marcus Garvey Park

E. 125th St.

Triborough Bridge

Riverside Park

Broadway

Amsterdam Ave.

Morningside Park

HARLEM

EAST HARLEM

Thomas Jefferson Park

E. 110th St. Recreation Pier

Cathedral Pkwy.

E. 110th St.

Lexington Ave.

Madison Ave.

Park Ave.

Wards Island Park

278

W. 106th St.

Columbus Ave.

Central Park West

Central Park

Fifth Ave.

E. 106th St.

Third Ave.

Second Ave.

First Ave.

FDR Dr.

East River Esplanade

West End Ave.

9A

W. 96th St.

W. 96th St.

UPPER WEST SIDE

Jacqueline Kennedy Onassis Reservoir

E. 96th St.

UPPER EAST SIDE

York Ave.

East River

QUEENS

Carl Schurz Park

N

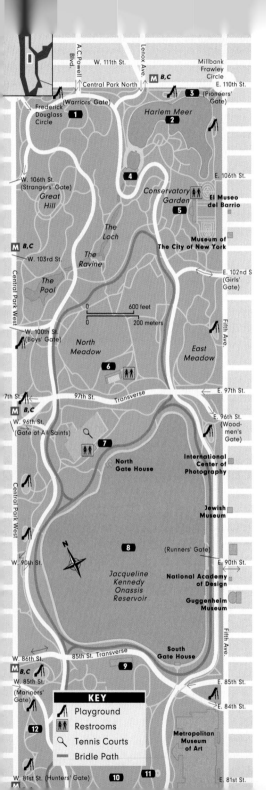

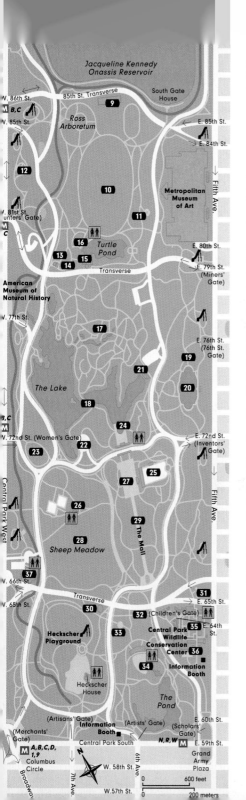

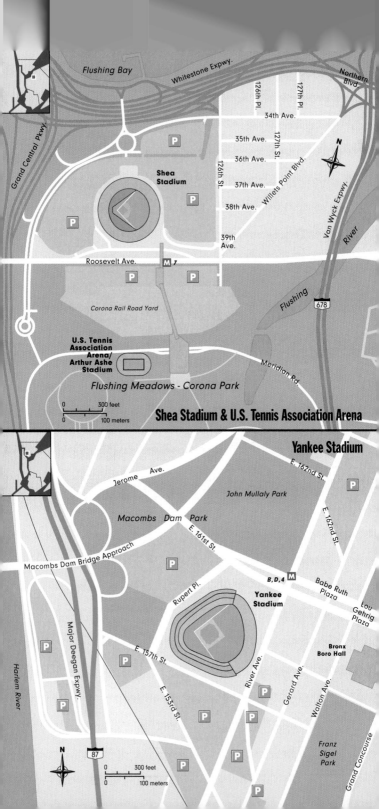

Shea Stadium & U.S. Tennis Association Arena

Flushing Bay

Whitestone Expwy.

Northern Blvd.

Grand Central Pkwy.

126th Pl.

127th Pl.

34th Ave.

35th Ave.

127th St.

36th Ave.

37th Ave.

Willets Point Blvd.

Van Wyck Expwy.

River

126th St.

Shea Stadium

P

P

P

P

38th Ave.

39th Ave.

Roosevelt Ave.

M 7

P

P

Flushing

678

Corona Rail Road Yard

U.S. Tennis Association Arena/ Arthur Ashe Stadium

Meridian Rd.

Flushing Meadows - Corona Park

N

0   300 feet
0   100 meters

Yankee Stadium

Jerome   Ave.

E. 162nd St.

John Mullaly Park

P

E. 162nd St.

Macombs   Dam   Park

E. 161st St.

Macombs Dam Bridge Approach

P

B, D, 4   M   Babe Ruth Plaza

Rupert Pl.

Yankee Stadium

Lou Gehrig Plaza

Major Deegan Expwy.

P

E. 157th St.

River Ave.

Gerard Ave.

Bronx Boro Hall

P

Harlem River

P

E. 153rd St.

P

P

P

Walton Ave.

Grand Concourse

Franz Sigel Park

N

87

0   300 feet
0   100 meters

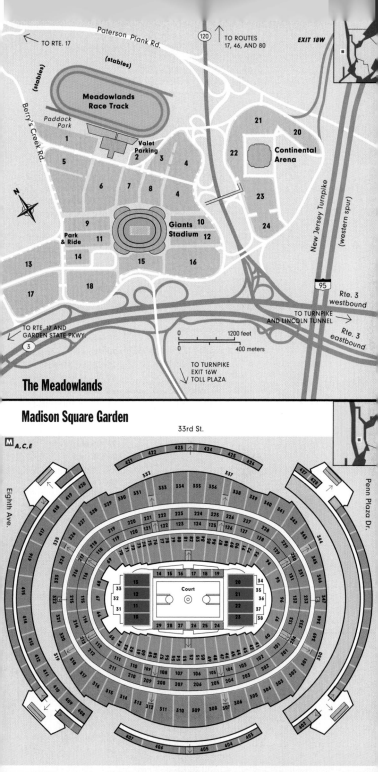

The Meadowlands

TO RTE. 17

Paterson Plank Rd.

120 ↑ TO ROUTES 17, 46, AND 80

EXIT 18W

(stables)

(stables)

Meadowlands
Race Track

Berry's Creek Rd.

Paddock
Park

1

Valet
Parking

5

2

3

4

6

7

8

4

9

Park
& Ride

11

10

Giants
Stadium

12

13

14

15

16

17

18

TO RTE. 17 AND
GARDEN STATE PKWY.

3

21

20

22

Continental
Arena

23

24

New Jersey Turnpike

(western spur)

95

Rte. 3
westbound

TO TURNPIKE
AND LINCOLN TUNNEL →

Rte. 3
eastbound

0   1200 feet
0   400 meters

TO TURNPIKE
EXIT 16W
TOLL PLAZA

Madison Square Garden

33rd St.

M A, C, E

Eighth Ave.

Penn Plaza Dr.

Court

31st St.

THE BRONX

W. 135th St.

Major Deegan Expwy.

278

Harlem River Dr.

E. 125th St.

Triborough Br.

Randalls Island

Broadway

Riverside Dr.

Henry Hudson Pkwy.

A.C. Powell Jr. Blvd.

Frederick Douglass Blvd.

Lenox Ave.

5th Ave.

Madison Ave.

Park Ave.

Lexington Ave.

3rd Ave.

2nd Ave.

E. 110th St.

E. 96th St.

Central Park West

Columbus Ave.

Amsterdam Ave.

Broadway

West End Ave.

W. 86th St.

E. 86th St.

1

Wards Island

QUEENS

E. 79th St.

2nd Ave.

3rd Ave.

1st Ave.

York Ave.

FDR Dr.

2

W. 72nd St.

6

Park Ave.

5th Ave.

E. 72nd St.

Roosevelt Island

7

Central Park West

Broadway

12

8 **9**

10 **16** **11**

13 **14** **18** **15** **17**

Queensboro Br.

W. 57th St.

20 **21** **19**

22 **23**

24

45

Lincoln Tunnel

W. 42nd St.

30

26

E. 42nd St.

Queens-Midtown Tunnel

495

9A

11th Ave.

10th Ave.

9th Ave.

8th Ave.

7th Ave.

Broadway

Ave. of the Americas

5th Ave.

Madison Ave.

Park Ave. S.

Lexington Ave.

3rd Ave.

2nd Ave.

1st Ave.

East River

27

W. 34th St.

28

29

West Side Hwy.

12th Ave.

11th Ave.

10th Ave.

9th Ave.

32

Madison Sq. Park

31

E. 23rd St.

W. 23rd St.

33 **37**

34

39 W. 14th St.

35

E. 14th St.

Ave. D

Ave. C

Ave. B

Ave. A

1st Ave.

2nd Ave.

3rd Ave.

38

36

Broadway

Hudson River

Greenwich St.

Washington St.

40

Washington Sq. Park

41

W. Houston St.

E. Houston St.

47

42

43

44

45

W. Broadway

Varick St.

Lafayette St.

Bowery

Orchard St.

Williamsburg Br.

46

Canal St.

Holland Tunnel

NEW JERSEY

N

Chambers St.

Broadway

49

Manhattan Br.

48

Wall St.

Brooklyn Br.

BROOKLYN

Brooklyn-Battery Tunnel

0 ___ 1 mile

0 ___ 1 km

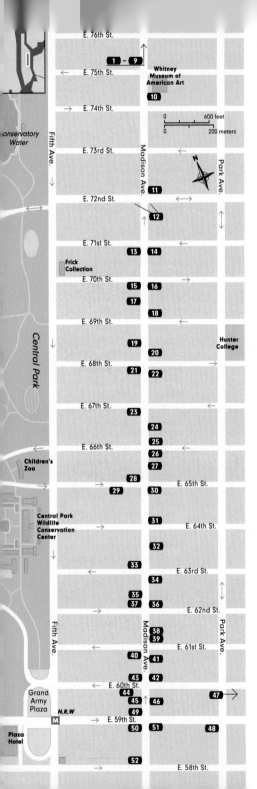

Listed by
Site Number

1 Wicker Garden's Baby
2 Crawford Doyle Booksellers
3 Alicia Mugetti
4 La Maison du Chocolat
5 Missoni
6 Vera Wang
7 Issey Miyake
8 Bang & Olufsen
9 Archivia
10 Christian Louboutin
11 Portantina
12 Polo/Polo Sport
13 Pierre Deux
14 Yves St Laurent
15 Chloé
16 Prada
17 Gucci
18 Pratesi
19 Dolce & Gabbana
20 Gianni Versace
21 JM Weston
22 Moschino
23 Emanuel Ungaro
24 La Perla
25 Fred Leighton
26 Krizia
27 Jean Paul Gaultier
28 Giorgio Armani
29 Mitchel London
30 Valentino
31 Chanel Jewelry
32 Erica Wilson
33 Givenchy
34 Timberland
35 Suzanne
36 Hermès
37 Marimekko
38 Georg Jensen
39 Sherry Lehmann Inc
40 Barneys NY
41 Cole-Haan
42 DKNY
43 Calvin Klein
44 Nicole Farhi
45 Tod's
46 Bottega Veneta
47 Diesel
48 Simon Pearce
49 Crate & Barrel
50 Bally of Switzerland
51 Baccarat
52 FAO Schwarz

Listed Alphabetically

Alicia Mugetti, 3.
999 Madison Ave ☎ 794-6186

Archivia Art Bookstore, 9.
1063 Madison Ave., 2nd fl. ☎ 439-9194

Baccarat, 51.
625 Madison Ave ☎ 826-4100

Bally of Switzerland, 50.
628 Madison Ave ☎ 751-9082

Bang & Olufsen, 8.
952 Madison Ave ☎ 879-6161

Barneys NY, 40.
660 Madison Ave ☎ 826-8900

Bottega Veneta, 46.
635 Madison Ave ☎ 371-5511

Calvin Klein, 43.
654 Madison Ave ☎ 292-9000

Chanel Jewelry, 31.
733 Madison Ave. ☎ 535-5828

Chloé, 15.
850 Madison Ave ☎ 717-8220

Christian Louboutin, 10.
941 Madison Ave ☎ 396-1884

Cole-Haan, 41.
667 Madison Ave ☎ 421-8440

Crate & Barrel, 49.
650 Madison Ave. ☎ 308-0011

Crawford Doyle Booksellers, 2.
1082 Madison Ave ☎ 288-6300

Diesel, 47.
770 Lexington Ave. ☎ 308-0055

DKNY, 42.
655 Madison Ave ☎ 223-3569

Dolce & Gabbana, 19.
825 Madison Ave ☎ 249-4100

Emanuel Ungaro, 23.
792 Madison Ave ☎ 249-4090

Erica Wilson, 32.
717 Madison Ave ☎ 832-7290

FAO Schwarz, 52.
767 Fifth Ave ☎ 644-9400

Fred Leighton, 25.
773 Madison Ave ☎ 288-1872

Georg Jensen, 38.
683 Madison Ave ☎ 759-6457

Gianni Versace, 20.
815 Madison Ave ☎ 744-6868

Giorgio Armani, 28.
760 Madison Ave ☎ 988-9191

Givenchy, 33.
710 Madison Ave ☎ 688-4338

Gucci, 17.
840 Madison Ave ☎ 717-2619

Hermès, 36.
691 Madison Ave ☎ 751-3181

Issey Miyake, 7.
992 Madison Ave ☎ 439-7822

Jean Paul Gaultier, 27.
759 Madison Ave ☎ 249-0235

JM Weston, 21.
812 Madison Ave ☎ 535-2100

Krizia, 26.
769 Madison Ave ☎ 879-1211

La Maison du Chocolat, 4.
1018 Madison Ave ☎ 744-7117

La Perla, 24.
777 Madison Ave ☎ 570-0050

Marimekko, 37.
698 Madison Ave ☎ 838-3842

Missoni, 5.
1009 Madison Ave ☎ 517-9339

Mitchel London Foods, 29.
22A E 65th St ☎ 737-2850

Moschino, 22.
803 Madison Ave. ☎ 639-9600

Nicole Farhi, 44.
10 E 60th St ☎ 223-8811

Pierre Deux, 13.
870 Madison Ave ☎ 570-9343

Polo/Polo Sport, 12.
867 Madison Ave ☎ 606-2100 and
888 Madison Ave ☎ 434-8000

Portantina, 11.
895 Madison Ave ☎ 472-0636

Prada, 16.
841 Madison Ave ☎ 327-4200

Pratesi, 18.
829 Madison Ave ☎ 288-2315

Sherry-Lehmann Inc, 39.
679 Madison Ave ☎ 838-7500

Simon Pearce, 48.
500 Park Ave. ☎ 421-8801

Suzanne, 35.
700 Madison Ave. 593-3232

Timberland, 34.
709 Madison Ave ☎ 754-0436

Tod's, 45. 650 Madison Ave ☎ 644-5945

Valentino, 30.
747 Madison Ave ☎ 772-6969

Vera Wang, 6.
991 Madison Ave ☎ 628-3400

Wicker Garden's Baby, 1.
1327 Madison Ave ☎ 410-2777

Yves St Laurent, 14.
855 Madison Ave ☎ 988-3821

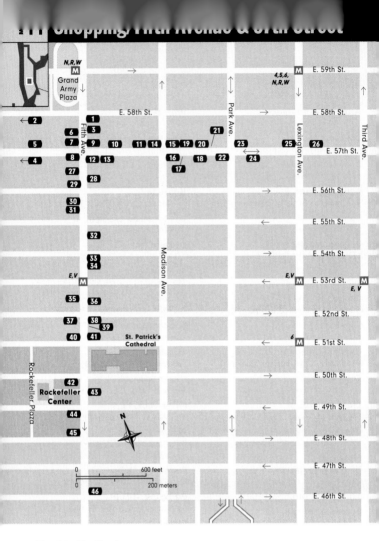

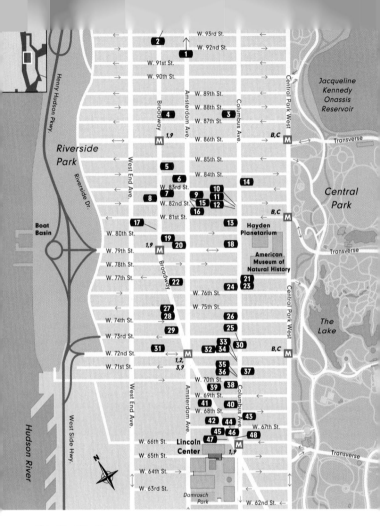

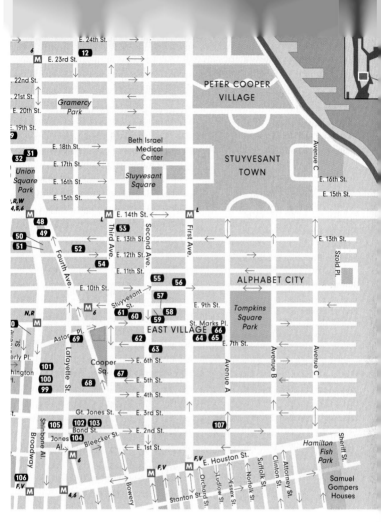

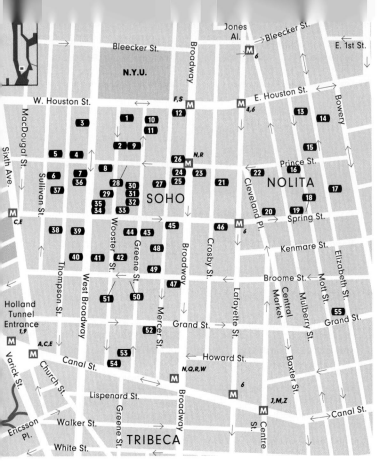

Listed by Site Number

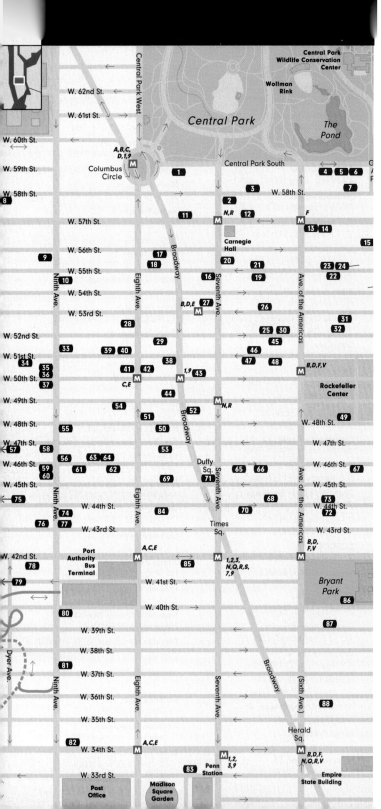

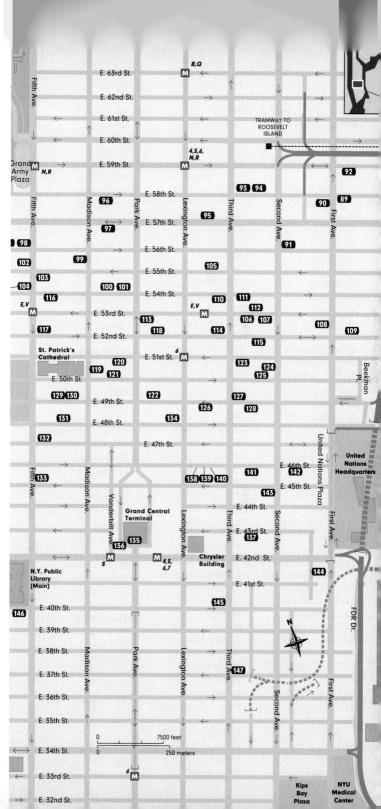

Listed by Site Number

Listed Alphabetically

Alain Ducasse NY, 3. 155 W 58th St
☎ 265-7300. French. $$$$

Aquavit, 104. 13 W 54th St
☎ 307-7311. Scandinavian. $$$$

Atlas, 5. 40 Central Park S
☎ 759-9191. Contemporary. $$$

Avra, 134. 141 E 48th St ☎ 759-8550.
Seafood. $$-$$$

Baldoria, 44. 249 W 49th St
☎ 582-0460. Italian. $$-$$$

Bali Nusa Indah, 59. 651 Ninth Ave
☎ 265-2200. Indonesian. $$

Barbetta, 63. 321 W 46th St
☎ 246-9171. Italian. $$-$$$

Beacon, 15. 25 W 56th St
☎ 332-0500. American. $$$-$$$$

Becco, 64. 355 W 46th St
☎ 397-7597. Italian. $$-$$$

Bellini, 115. 208 E 52nd St
☎ 308-0830. Italian. $$$

Ben Benson's, 30. 123 W 52nd St
☎ 581-8888. Steak. $$$

Bienvenue, 130. 21 E 36th St.
☎ 684-0215. French. $$

Brasserie, 113. 100 E 53rd St
☎ 751-4840. French. $$-$$$

Bryant Park Cafe, 86. 25 W 40th St
☎ 840-6500. American. $$-$$$

Bryant Park Grill, 86. 25 W 40th St
☎ 840-6500. American. $$-$$$

Café Un Deux Trois, 68. 123 W 44th St
☎ 354-4148. French. $$

Caffe Cielo, 28. 881 Eighth Ave
☎ 246-9555. Italian. $$

Carnegie Deli, 16. 854 Seventh Ave
☎ 757-2245. Deli. $$

Cellini, 101. 65 E 54th St ☎ 751-1555.
Italian. $$-$$$

Chez Josephine, 78. 414 W 42nd St
☎ 594-1925. International. $$$

Chimichurri Grill, 74. 606 Ninth Ave
☎ 586-8655. Argentine. $$

Chin Chin, 128. 216 E 49th St
☎ 888-4555. Chinese. $$-$$$

China Grill, 31. 52 W 53rd St
☎ 333-7788. Pan-Asian. $$$

Churrascaria Plataforma, 54.
316 W 49th St ☎ 245-0505.
Brazilian. $$$

Cité, 48. 120 W 51st St
☎ 956-7100. Steak. $$$-$$$$

Colbeh, 87. 43 W 39th St
☎ 354-8181.
Middle Eastern. $-$$

Columbus Bakery, 108. 957 First Ave
☎ 421-0334. Light Fare. $

Cupcake Cafe, 80. 522 Ninth Ave
☎ 465-1530. Bakery/Cafe. $

D'Artagnan, 139. 152 E 46th St
☎ 687-0300. French. $$-$$$

Dawat, 93. 210 E 58th St
☎ 355-7555. Indian. $$

db bistro moderne, 72. 55 W 44th St
☎ 391-5353. French. $$$

Delta Grill, 55. 700 Ninth Ave
☎ 956-0934. Cajun. $-$$

District, 66. 130 W 46th St
☎ 485-2999. American. $$$-$$$$

Esca, 77. 402 W 43rd St ☎ 564-7272.
Seafood. $$$

Estiatorio Milos, 21. 125 W 55th St
☎ 245-7400. Greek. $$$-$$$$

Felidia, 94. 243 E 58th St ☎ 758-1479.
Italian. $$-$$$$

5757, 97. 57 E 57th St ☎ 758-5757.
Contemporary. $$-$$$$

Firebird, 56. 365 W 46th St
☎ 586-0244. Russian. $$$-$$$$

Five, 102. 700 Fifth Ave
☎ 903-3918. Eclectic. $$$$

Fontana di Trevi, 12. 151 W 57th St
☎ 247-5683. Italian. $$

44 & X Hell's Kitchen, 75.
622 Tenth Ave ☎ 977-1170.
Contemporary. $$

Four Seasons, 118. 99 E 52nd St
☎ 754-9494. American. $$$$

Frankie & Johnny's, 69. 269 W 45th St
☎ 997-9494. American. $$-$$$

Gallagher's, 29. 228 W 52nd St
☎ 245-5336. Steakhouse. $$-$$$$

Grand Sichuan International, 36.
745 Ninth Ave ☎ 582-2288. Chinese. $-$$

Greek Kitchen, 8. 889 Tenth Ave
☎ 581-4300. Greek. $$

Gustavino's, 92. 409 E 59th St
☎ 980-2455. Eclectic. $$-$$$$

Hallo Berlin, 34. 402 W 51st St
☎ 541-6248. German. $

$$$$ = *over $32* $$$ = *$25-$32* $$ = *$15-$24* $ = *under $15*
Based on cost per person for an entrée.

Listed Alphabetically (cont.)

Hard Rock Cafe, 11.
221 W 57th St ☎ 489–6565.
American. $-$$

Hatsuhana, 131. 17 E 48th St
☎ 355–3345. Japanese. $$$-$$$$

Heartbeat, 126. 149 E 49th St ☎ 407–2900.
Contemporary. $$-$$$$

Hell's Kitchen, 58. 679 Ninth Ave
☎ 977–1588. Eclectic. $$

Houston's, 110. 153 E 53rd St
☎ 888–3828. American. $$

Hurley's, 50. 232 W 48th St
☎ 765–8981. American. $$

Il Nido, 112. 251 E 53rd St
☎ 753–8450. Italian. $$$$

Ilo, 146. 40 W 40th St ☎ 642–2255.
Contemporary. $$$-$$$$

Inagiku, 122. 111 E 49th St
☎ 355–0440. Japanese. $$$-$$$$

Island Burgers & Shakes, 33.
766 Ninth Ave ☎ 307–7934. American. $

John's Pizzeria, 84. 260 W 44th St
☎ 391–7560. Pizza. $-$$

Josie's, 147. 565 Third Ave
☎ 490–1558. Vegetarian. $-$$

JUdson Grill, 25. 152 W 52nd St
☎ 582–5252. American. $$$-$$$$

Keen's, 88. 72 W 36th St ☎ 947–3636.
Steak. $$$

Kuruma Zushi, 132. 7 E 47th St
☎ 317–2802. Japanese. $$-$$$$

La Caravelle, 24. 33 W 55th St
☎ 586–4252. French. $$$$

La Côte Basque, 22. 60 W 55th St
☎ 688–6525. French. $$$$

La Grenouille, 117. 3 E 52nd St
☎ 752–1495. French. $$$$

La Locanda, 37. 737 Ninth Ave
☎ 258–2900. Italian. $$-$$$

Le Bernardin, 46. 155 W 51st St
☎ 489–1515. French. $$$$

Le Cirque 2000, 119. 455 Madison Ave
☎ 303–7788. French. $$$$

Le Colonial, 95. 149 E 57th St
☎ 752–0808. Vietnamese. $$-$$$

Le Madeleine, 76. 403 W 43rd St
☎ 246–2993. French. $$

Le Marais, 65. 150 W 46th St
☎ 869–0900. French/Kosher. $$-$$$

Le Perigord, 109. 405 E 52nd St
☎ 755–6244. French. $$$$

Le Rivage, 61. 340 W 46th St
☎ 765–7374. French. $$-$$$

Lespinasse, 103. 2 E 55th St
☎ 339–6719. French. $$$$

L'Impero, 144. 45 Tudor City Pl
☎ 599–5045. Italian. $$$

Lundy's Midtown, 43. 205 W 50th St
☎ 856–6167. American. $$-$$$$

Lutèce, 125. 249 E 50th St
☎ 752–2225. French. $$$$

Maloney & Porcelli, 121. 37 E 50th St
☎ 750–2233. Contemporary. $$$-$$$$

Mangia, 14. 50 W 57th St
☎ 582–3061. Italian. $

Manhattan Ocean Club, 7.
57 W 58th St ☎ 371–7777. Seafood. $$$

Maple Garden, 107. 236 E 53rd St
☎ 759–8260. Chinese. $-$$

March, 89. 405 E 58th St ☎ 754–6272.
Contemporary. $$$$

Marichu, 142. 342 E 46th St
☎ 370–1866. Spanish. $$

Market Cafe, 81. 496 Ninth Ave
☎ 564–7350. American. $

Mars 2112, 38. 1633 Broadway
☎ 582–2112. Eclectic. $$

Meskerem, 57. 468 W 47th St
☎ 664–0520. Ethiopian. $

**Michael Jordan's The Steak House
NYC, 136.** 23 Vanderbilt Ave
☎ 655–2300. Steak. $$$-$$$$

Mickey Mantle's, 4. 42 Central Park S
☎ 688–7777. American. $$

Molyvos, 20. 871 Seventh Ave
☎ 582–7500. Greek. $$-$$$

Montparnasse, 123. 230 E 51st St
☎ 758–6633. French. $$-$$$

Morton's of Chicago, 133.
551 Fifth Ave ☎ 972–3315. Steak. $$$$

Nanni's, 138. 146 E 46th St
☎ 697–4161. Italian. $$-$$$

Nick & Stef's Steakhouse, 83.
9 Penn Plaza ☎ 563–4444.
Steak. $$$-$$$$

Nippon, 114. 155 E 52nd St
☎ 355–9020. Japanese. $$$

Nirvana, 6. 30 Central Park S
☎ 486–5700. Indian. $$$

Nocello, 18. 257 W 55th St
☎ 713–0224. Italian. $$

Noche, 52. 1604 Broadway
☎ 541–7070. Latin. $$-$$$

Oceana, 100. 55 E 54th St
☎ 759-5941. Seafood. $$$$

Onigashima, 23. 43-45 W 55th St
☎ 541-7145. Japanese. $$-$$$

Orso, 62. 322 W 46th St ☎ 489-7212.
Italian. $$$

Osteria del Circo, 19. 120 W 55th St
☎ 265-3636. Italian. $$-$$$

Oyster Bar, 135. Grand Central Terminal
☎ 490-6650. Seafood. $-$$$

Palm, 143. 837 Second Ave
☎ 687-2953. Steak. $$-$$$$

Patroon, 140. 160 E 46th St
☎ 883-7373. American. $$$-$$$$

Patsy's, 17. 236 W 56th St
☎ 247-3491. Italian. $$-$$$

Petrossian, 2. 182 W 58th St
☎ 245-2214. Continental. $$$

Picasso, 91. 303 E 56th St ☎ 759-8767.
Spanish. $$-$$$

Pierre au Tunnel, 53. 250 W 47th St
☎ 575-1220. French. $$-$$$

Pigalle, 51. 790 Eighth Ave
☎ 489-2233. French. $-$$

Planet Hollywood, 71. 1540 Broadway
☎ 333-7827. American. $$

Puttanesca, 9. 859 Ninth Ave
☎ 581-4177. Italian. $$

Remi, 26. 145 W 53rd St ☎ 581-4242.
Italian. $$$

René Pujol, 39. 321 W 51st St
☎ 246-3023. French. $$$-$$$$

Restaurant Above, 85. 234 W 42nd St
☎ 642-2626. Pan-Asian. $$$

Rice & Beans, 42. 744 Ninth Ave
☎ 265-4444. Brazilian. $

Rosa Mexicano, 90. 1063 First Ave
☎ 753-7407. Mexican. $$-$$$

Rue 57, 13. 60 W 57th St
☎ 307-5656. French/Japanese. $$

Ruth's Chris Steakhouse, 47.
148 W 51st St ☎ 245-9600.
Steak. $$$-$$$$

San Domenico, 1. 240 Central Park S
☎ 265-5959. Italian. $$-$$$

San Pietro, 116. 18 E 54th St
☎ 753-9015. Italian. $$$-$$$$

Shaan, 49. Rockefeller Ctr, 57 W 48th St
☎ 977-8400. Indian. $-$$$

Shallots, 99. 550 Madison Ave
☎ 833-7800. Kosher. $$$-$$$$

Shun Lee Palace, 105.
155 E 55th St
☎ 371-8844. Chinese. $$$

Smith & Wollensky, 127.
797 Third Ave
☎ 753-1530. Steak. $$$-$$$$

Solera, 106. 216 E 53rd St
☎ 644-1166. Spanish. $$$

Soul Fixins', 82. 371 W 34th St
☎ 736-1345. Soul. $

Sparks Steak House, 141. 210 E 46th St
☎ 687-4855. Steak. $$-$$$$

Stage Deli, 27. 834 Seventh Ave
☎ 245-7850. Deli. $-$$

Sushi Yasuda, 137. 204 E 43rd St
☎ 972-1001. Japanese. $$-$$$

Sushiden, 129. 19 E 49th St
☎ 758-2700. Japanese. $$$

Tao, 96. 42 E 58th St ☎ 888-2288.
Pan-Asian. $$-$$$

Tout Va Bien, 40. 311 W 51st St
☎ 265-0190. French. $$

Town, 98. 15 W 56th St ☎ 582-4445.
Contemporary. $$$-$$$$.

Triomphe, 73. 49 W 44th St
☎ 453-4233. French. $$$

Tse Yang, 120. 34 E 51st St
☎ 688-5447. Chinese. $$$-$$$$

Tuscan Steak, 145. 622 Third Ave
☎ 404-1700. Steak. $$$-$$$$

21 Club, 32. 21 W 52nd St
☎ 582-7200. American. $$$$

Uncle Nick's, 35. 747 Ninth Ave
☎ 245-7992. Greek. $-$$

Via Brasil, 67. 34 W 46th St
☎ 997-1158. Brazilian. $$

Victor's Café, 45. 236 W 52nd St
☎ 586-7714. Cuban. $-$$$

Vintage, 41. 753 Ninth Ave
☎ 581-4655. Contemporary. $$-$$$

Virgil's Real BBQ, 70. 152 W 44th St
☎ 921-9494. Barbecue. $-$$

Vong, 111. 200 E 54th St ☎ 486-9592.
Pan-Asian. $$-$$$$

Vynl, 10. 824 Ninth Ave ☎ 974-2003.
Eclectic. $-$$

World Yacht Cruises, 79. Pier 81,
W 41st St ☎ 630-8100.
Continental. $$$$

Zarela, 124. 953 Second Ave
☎ 644-6740. Mexican. $$

Zen Palate, 60. 663 Ninth Ave
☎ 582-1669. Vegetarian. $-$$

$$$$ = *over $32* $$$ = *$25-$32* $$ = *$15-$24* $ = *under $15*
Based on cost per person for an entrée.

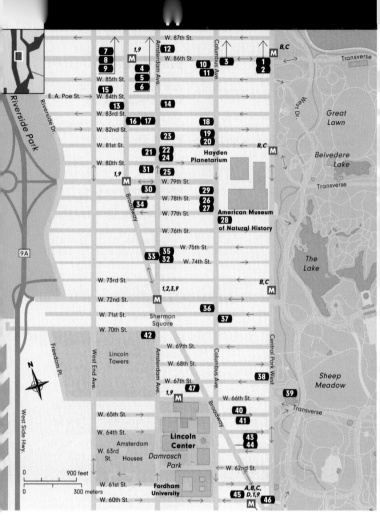

Listed by Site Number

Listed Alphabetically

AIX, 7. 2398 Broadway
☎ 874-7400. French. $$$

Alouette, 9. 2588 Broadway
☎ 222-6808. French. $$

Artie's Delicatessen, 16.
2290 Broadway ☎ 579-5959. Deli. $

Avenue, 11. 520 Columbus Ave
☎ 579-3194. French. $$-$$$

Barney Greengrass, 12.
541 Amsterdam Ave ☎ 724-4707.
Deli/Jewish. $

Café con Leche, 21. 424 Amsterdam
Ave ☎ 595-0936. Latin. $

Café des Artistes, 38. 1 W 67th St
☎ 877-3500. Continental. $$-$$$$

Café Frida, 26. 368 Columbus Ave
☎ 712-2929. Mexican. $-$$

Café Luxembourg, 42. 200 W 70th St
☎ 873-7411. French. $$-$$$

Calle Ocho, 20. 446 Columbus Ave
☎ 873-5025. Latin. $$-$$$

Carmine's, 8. 2450 Broadway
☎ 362-2200. Italian. $$-$$$$

Charles' Southern Style Chicken, 1.
2841 Eighth Ave ☎ 926-4313. Soul. $

Columbus Bakery, 18. 474 Columbus Ave
☎ 724-6880. Light Fare. $

Edgar's Cafe, 15. 255 W 84th St
☎ 496-6126. Dessert. $

EJ's Luncheonette, 23. 447 Amsterdam Ave
☎ 873-3444. American. $

Fiorello's, 44. 1900 Broadway
☎ 595-5330. Italian. $$-$$$

Fred's, 17. 476 Amsterdam Ave
☎ 579-3076. American. $-$$

Gabriela's, 5. 685 Amsterdam Ave
☎ 961-0574. Mexican. $-$$

Gabriela's, 35. 311 Amsterdam Ave
☎ 875-8532. Mexican. $-$$

Gabriel's, 45. 11 W 60th St
☎ 956-4600. Italian. $$-$$$

Gennaro, 6. 665 Amsterdam Ave
☎ 665-5348. Italian. $

Good Enough to Eat, 14.
483 Amsterdam Ave
☎ 496-0163. American. $-$$

Haru, 22. 433 Amsterdam Ave
☎ 579-5655. Japanese. $$

Isabella's, 28. 359 Columbus Ave
☎ 724-2100. Mediterranean. $$

Jean-Georges, 46.
1 Central Park W
☎ 299-3900. French. $$$$

John's Pizzeria, 41. 48 W 65th St
☎ 721-7001. Italian. $

Josephina, 44. 1900 Broadway
☎ 799-1000. American. $$

Josie's, 33. 300 Amsterdam Ave
☎ 769-1212. Vegetarian. $-$$

La Grolla, 25. 413 Amsterdam Ave
☎ 496-0890. Italian. $-$$

La Mirabelle, 10. 102 W 86th St
☎ 496-0458. French. $$-$$$

Ocean Grill, 29. 384 Columbus Ave
☎ 579-2300. Seafood. $$

Ollie's, 47. 1991 Broadway
☎ 595-8181. Chinese. $-$$

Ouest, 13. 2315 Broadway
☎ 580-8700. Contemporary. $$-$$$

Pampa, 4. 768 Amsterdam Ave
☎ 865-2929. Steak. $-$$

Pasha, 37. 70 W 71st St
☎ 579-8751. Turkish. $$

Penang, 36. 240 Columbus Ave
☎ 769-3988. Malaysian. $-$$

Picholine, 43. 35 W 64th St
☎ 724-8585. French. $$$-$$$$

Rain, 19. 100 W 82nd St
☎ 501-0776. Pan-Asian. $-$$

Ruby Foo's Dim Sum Palace, 34.
2182 Broadway ☎
724-6700. Pan-Asian. $-$$$

Sarabeth's Kitchen, 24. 423 Amsterdam
Ave ☎ 496-6280. American. $-$$

Savann, 31. 414 Amsterdam Ave
☎ 580-0202. French. $$

Shark Bar, 32. 307 Amsterdam Ave
☎ 874-8500. Southern. $-$$$

Shun Lee West, 40. 43 W 65th St
☎ 595-8895. Chinese. $$-$$$

Spazzia, 27. 366 Columbus Ave
☎ 799-0150. Italian. $$

Sylvia's, 2. 328 Lenox Ave
☎ 996-0660. Soul. $$

Tavern on the Green, 39.
Central Park W & 67th St
☎ 873-3200. Contemporary. $$-$$$$

Terrace, 3. 400 W 119th St
☎ 666-9490. French. $$$-$$$$

Two Two Two, 30. 222 W 79th St
☎ 799-0400. Contemporary. $$$-$$$$

$$$$ = *over $32* $$$ = *$25-$32* $$ = *$15-$24* $ = *under $15*
Based on cost per person for an entrée.

Listed Alphabetically

Atlantic Grill, 26. 1337 Third Ave
☎ 988-9200. Seafood. $$

Aureole, 41. 34 E 61st St ☎ 319-1660.
Contemporary. $$$$

Bravo Gianni, 39. 230 E 63rd St
☎ 752-7272. Italian. $$$

Butterfield 81, 11. 170 E 81st St
☎ 288-1700. American. $$-$$$

Café Boulud, 22. 20 E 76th St
☎ 772-2600. French. $$$-$$$$

Carlyle Restaurant, 20. Carlyle Hotel,
35 E 76th St ☎ 744-1600. French. $$$$

Candle Cafe, 31. 1307 Third Ave
☎ 472-0970. Vegan. $-$$

Canyon Road, 24. 1470 First Ave
☎ 734-1600. Southwestern. $$

Centolire, 9. 1167 Madison Ave
☎ 734-7711. Italian. $$$

Circus, 47. 808 Lexington Ave
☎ 223-2965. Brazilian. $$-$$$

Comfort Diner, 4. 142 E 86st St
☎ 426-8600. Diner. $

Daniel, 43. 60 E 65th St ☎ 288-0033.
French. $$$$

Dining Room, 19. 154 E 79th St
☎ 327-2500. American. $$-$$$

E.A.T., 15. 1064 Madison Ave
☎ 772-0022. Bakery. $

Emily's, 1. 1325 Fifth Ave ☎ 996-1212.
Southern. $-$$

Etats-Unis, 10. 242 E 81st St
☎ 517-8826. Eclectic. $$$

JG Melon, 29. 1291 Third Ave
☎ 744-0585. American. $-$$

Jo Jo, 40. 160 E 64th St ☎ 223-5656.
French. $$-$$$

Lenox, 33. 1278 Third Ave ☎ 772-0404.
American $$-$$$

Luca, 7. 1712 First Ave ☎ 987-9260.
Italian. $$

Lusardi's, 27. 1494 Second Ave
☎ 249-2020. Italian. $$$

Manhattan Grille, 38. 1161 First Ave
☎ 888-6556. Steak. $$-$$$$

Mark's Restaurant, 16. 25 E 77th St
☎ 879-1864. Continental. $$$-$$$$

Maya, 37. 1191 First Ave ☎ 585-1818.
Mexican. $$

Mezzaluna, 30. 1295 Third Ave
☎ 535-9600. Italian. $$-$$$

Mocca, 14. 1588 Second Ave
☎ 734-6470. Hungarian. $-$$

Nicole's, 46. 10 E 60th St
☎ 223-2288. Contemporary.
$$-$$$

Orsay, 21. 1057-1059 Lexington Ave
☎ 517-6400. French. $$-$$$$

Pamir, 34. 1437 Second Ave
☎ 734-3791. Afghan. $$

Park Avenue Café, 42. 100 E 63rd St
☎ 644-1900. American. $$$-$$$$

Payard Patisserie & Bistro, 32.
1032 Lexington Ave ☎ 717-5252.
French. $$-$$$

Persepolis, 35. 1423 Second Ave
☎ 535-1100. Persian. $$

Pio Pio, 8. 1746 First Ave ☎ 426-5800.
Peruvian. $

Post House, 44. 28 E 63rd St
☎ 935-2888. Steak. $$$$

Rain, 48. 1059 Third Ave
☎ 223-3669. Pan-Asian. $-$$

Saigon Grill, 6. 1700 Second Ave
☎ 996-4600. Vietnamese. $

Sarabeth's, 3. 1295 Madison Ave
☎ 410-7335. American. $-$$

Serafina Fabulous Pizza, 17.
1022 Madison Ave ☎ 734-2676.
Pizza. $-$$

Serendipity 3, 45. 225 E 60th St
☎ 838-3531. American. $-$$

Sistina, 13. 1555 Second Ave
☎ 861-7660. Italian. $$-$$$

Sushi of Gari, 28. 402 E 78th St
☎ 517-5340. Japanese. $-$$$

Table d'Hote, 2. 44 E 92nd St
☎ 348-8125. French. $$$

Taperia Madrid, 25. 1471 Second Ave
☎ 794-2923. Tapas. $$

Trata, 36. 1331 Second Ave
☎ 535-3800. Greek. $$$

Vermicelli, 23. 1492 Second Ave
☎ 288-8868. Vietnamese. $

Viand, 18. 1011 Madison Ave
☎ 249-8250. Coffee Shop. $

Wu Liang Ye, 5. 215 E 86th St
☎ 534-8899. Chinese. $-$$

Zócalo, 12. 174 E 82nd St ☎ 717-7772.
Mexican. $$

$$$$ = *over $32* $$$ = *$25-$32* $$ = *$15-$24* $ = *under $15*
Based on cost per person for an entrée.

Listed by Site Number

1	Gam Mee Ok	26	Olives NY
2	Mandoo Bar	27	Yama
3	Hangawi	28	Craft
4	Kang Suh	29	Mesa Grill
5	Artisanal	30	Union Square Café
6	Water Club	31	Republic
7	Biricchino	32	Blue Water Grill
8	Seven	33	Cal's
9	Les Halles	34	AZ
10	Pongal	35	Lola
11	Turkish Kitchen	36	Periyali
12	Park Bistro	37	Eisenberg's Sandwich Shop
13	Eleven Madison Park	38	City Bakery
13	Tabla	39	Da Umberto
14	I Trulli	40	Gascogne
15	Fleur de Sel	41	Rocking Horse Cafe
16	Beppe	42	Maroons
17	Tamarind	43	Bright Food Shop
18	Union Pacific	44	Chelsea Bistro
19	Bolo	45	Parish & Co
20	Kitchen 22	46	Half King
21	Veritas	47	Bottino
22	Gramercy Tavern	48	The Red Cat
23	Patria	49	Grand Sichuan
24	Chicama		
25	Pipa		

$$$$ = *over $32* $$$ = *$25-$32* $$ = *$15-$24* $ = *under $15*
Based on cost per person for an entrée.

Listed by Site Number

$$$$ = *over $32* $$$ = *$25-$32* $$ = *$15-$24* $ = *under $15*
Based on cost per person for an entrée.

Listed Alphabetically (cont.)

Gotham Bar & Grill, 8.
12 E 12th St ☎ 620-4020.
Contemporary. $$$-$$$$

Grange Hall, 32. 50 Commerce St
☎ 924-5246. Cajun/Creole. $-$$

Great Jones Cafe, 61. 54 Great
Jones St ☎ 674-9304. Cajun. $

Great New York Noodletown, 124.
28 ½ Bowery ☎ 349-0923.
Chinese. $-$$

The Harrison, 118. 355 Greenwich St
☎ 274-9310. Contemporary $$-$$$$

Hasaki, 64. 210 E 9th St
☎ 473-3327. Japanese. $$-$$$

Haveli, 84. 100 Second Ave
☎ 982-0533. Indian. $-$$

Holy Basil, 67. 149 Second Ave
☎ 460-5557. Thai. $-$$

Home, 25. 20 Cornelia St
☎ 243-9579. American. $$

Honmura An, 58. 170 Mercer St
☎ 334-5253. Japanese. $-$$$

I Coppi, 74. 432 E 9th St
☎ 254-2263. Italian. $-$$

Il Bagatto, 95. 192 E 2nd St
☎ 228-0977. Italian. $-$$

Il Buco, 60. 47 Bond St ☎ 533-1932.
Italian. $$-$$$

Il Mulino, 34. 86 W 3rd St
☎ 673-3783. Italian. $$$-$$$$

'Ino, 41. 21 Bedford St
☎ 989-5769. Italian. $-$$

Japonica, 11. 100 University Pl
☎ 243-7752. Japanese. $$-$$$

Jean Claude, 44. 137 Sullivan St
☎ 475-9232. French. $$

Jefferson, 16. 121 W 10th St
☎ 255-3333. American. $$-$$$

Jing Fong, 129. 20 Elizabeth St
☎ 964-5256. Chinese. $

Joe's Shanghai, 123. 9 Pell St.
☎ 233-8888. Chinese. $-$$

John's Pizzeria, 35. 278 Bleecker St
☎ 243-1680. Pizza. $

Junno's, 40. 64 Downing St
☎ 627-7995. Korean. $-$$

Katz's Delicatessen, 91.
205 E Houston St ☎ 254-2246. Deli. $

Kitchenette, 136. 80 W Broadway
☎ 267-6740. American. $-$$

La Metairie, 15. 189 W 10th St
☎ 989-0343. French. $$-$$$

La Paella, 65. 214 E 9th St
☎ 598-4321. Spanish. $$

La Palapa, 76. 77 St Mark's Pl
☎ 777-2537. Mexican. $-$$

Layla, 113. 211 W Broadway
☎ 431-0700. Middle Eastern. $$$

Le Gamin, 43. 50 MacDougal St
☎ 254-8409. French. $

Le Jardin, 103. 25 Cleveland Pl
☎ 343-9599. French. $$-$$$

Les Halles, 141. 15 John St
☎ 285-8585. French. $$-$$$

Lombardi's, 107. 32 Spring St
☎ 941-7994. Pizza. $-$$

Lupa, 37. 170 Thompson St
☎ 982-5089. Italian. $$

Macelleria, 3. 48 Gansevoort
☎ 741-2555. Italian. $$-$$$

Magnolia Bakery, 13. 401 Bleecker St
☎ 462-2572. Bakery. $

Malatesta Trattoria, 29.
649 Washington St ☎ 741-1207.
Italian. $-$$

Mary's Fish Camp, 14. 64 Charles St
☎ 646/486-2185. Seafood. $$

Mekka, 94. 14 Ave A ☎ 475-8500.
Soul/Caribbean. $$

Mercer Kitchen, 53. 99 Prince St
☎ 966-5454. Contemporary. $$-$$$

Merge, 17. 142 W 10th St
☎ 691-7757. American. $$

Mexicana Mama, 27. 525 Hudson St
☎ 924-4119. Mexican. $-$$

Mezzogiorno, 50. 195 Spring St
☎ 334-2112. Italian. $$

Mingala, 73. 21-23 E 7th St
☎ 529-3656. Burmese. $-$$

Miracle Grill, 78. 112 First Ave
☎ 254-2353. Southwestern. $-$$

Mogador Cafe, 77. 101 St Marks Pl
☎ 677-2226. Moroccan. $

Montrachet, 112. 239 W Broadway
☎ 219-2777. French. $$$

Moran's, 144. 103 Washington St
☎ 732-2020. Steak/Seafood. $$$$

Nha Trang, 120. 87 Baxter St
☎ 233-5948. Vietnamese. $

Nobu, 117. 105 Hudson St
☎ 219-0500. Japanese. $$-$$$

Nyonya, 108. 194 Grand St
☎ 343-6701. Malaysian. $

Odeon, 132. 145 W Broadway
☎ 233-0507. Bistro. $$-$$$

One If By Land, Two If By Sea, 20.
17 Barrow St ☎ 228-0822. Continental. $$$$

Otafuku, 66. 236 E 9th St
☎ 387-8869. Japanese. $

Palacincka, 111. 28 Grand St
☎ 625-0362. Eclectic. $

Pastis, 2. 9 Ninth Ave ☎ 929-4844.
French. $$-$$$$

Pearl Oyster Bar, 23. 18 Cornelia St
☎ 691-8211. Seafood. $$-$$$

Peasant, 101. 194 Elizabeth St
☎ 965-9511. Italian. $$

Petite Abeille, 31. 466 Hudson St
☎ 741-6479. Belgian. $-$$

Philip Marie, 12. 569 Hudson St
☎ 242-6200. New American. $$

Pica's, 116. 349 Greenwich St
☎ 343-0700. Portuguese. $$-$$$

Ping's Seafood, 122. 27 Mott St
☎ 602-9988. Chinese. $-$$

Pink Tea Cup, 28. 42 Grove St
☎ 807-6755. Soul. $

Pisces, 79. 95 Ave A
☎ 260-6660. Seafood. $-$$

Pó, 22. 31 Cornelia St
☎ 645-2189. Italian. $$

Provence, 47. 38 MacDougal St
☎ 475-7500. French. $$-$$$

Prune, 89. 54 E 1st St
☎ 677-6221. American. $$-$$$

Radio Perfecto, 70. 190 Ave B
☎ 477-3366. American. $

Rai Rai Ken, 69. 214 E 10th St
☎ 477-7030. Japanese. $

Raga, 81. 433 E 6th St
☎ 388-0957. Indian. $-$$

Raoul's, 45. 180 Prince St
☎ 966-3518. French. $$-$$$

Rialto, 97. 265 Elizabeth St
☎ 334-7900. American. $-$$

Rice, 104. 227 Mott St
☎ 226-5775. Eclectic. $

Roy's New York, 139.
130 Washington St ☎ 266-6262.
Pan-Asian. $$$

Salaam Bombay, 130.
319 Greenwich St ☎ 226-9400.
Indian. $$-$$$

Sammy's Roumanian, 106.
157 Chrystie St ☎ 673-0330.
Eastern European. $$$

Savoy, 99. 70 Prince St
☎ 219-8570. Contemporary. $$-$$$

Second Ave Deli, 71. 156 Second Ave
☎ 677-0606. Deli. $$-$$$

71 Clinton Fresh Food, 96.
71 Clinton St ☎ 614-6960.
Contemporary. $$-$$$

Shopsin's General Store, 33.
54 Carmine St ☎ 924-5160. Eclectic. $

Soho Steak, 46. 90 Thompson St
☎ 226-0602. French. $$

Strip House, 10. 13 E 12th St
☎ 328-0000. Steak. $$$

Surya, 18. 302 Bleecker St
☎ 807-7777. Indian. $$

Sweet 'n' Tart Restaurant, 119.
76 Mott St ☎ 334-8088. Chinese. $-$$

Takahachi, 80. 85 Ave A
☎ 505-6524. Japanese. $-$$

Tasting Room, 93. 72 E 1st St
☎ 358-7831. Contemporary. $$-$$$

Thailand, 121. 106 Bayard St
☎ 349-3132. Thai. $-$$

Tomoe Sushi, 38. 172 Thompson St
☎ 777-9346. Japanese. $$

Tribeca Grill, 114. 375 Greenwich St
☎ 941-3900. Contemporary. $$-$$$

2 West, 145. 2 West St (Ritz Carlton)
☎ 917/790-2525. American. $$$-$$$$

Veselka, 72. 144 Second Ave
☎ 228-9682. East European. $

Viet-Nam, 125. 11-13 Doyers St
☎ 693-0725. Vietnamese. $

Villa Mosconi, 36. 69 MacDougal St
☎ 673-0390. Italian. $$

Yaffa Cafe, 75. 97 St Mark's Pl
☎ 674-9302. Vegetarian. $-$$

Wallsé, 26. 344 W 11th St
☎ 352-2300. Austrian. $$-$$$

Woo Lae Oak, 57. 148 Mercer St
☎ 925-8200. Korean. $$

Zoë, 55. 90 Prince St
☎ 966-6722. American. $$$

$$$$ = *over $32* $$$ = *$25-$32* $$ = *$15-$24* $ = *under $15*
Based on cost per person for an entrée.

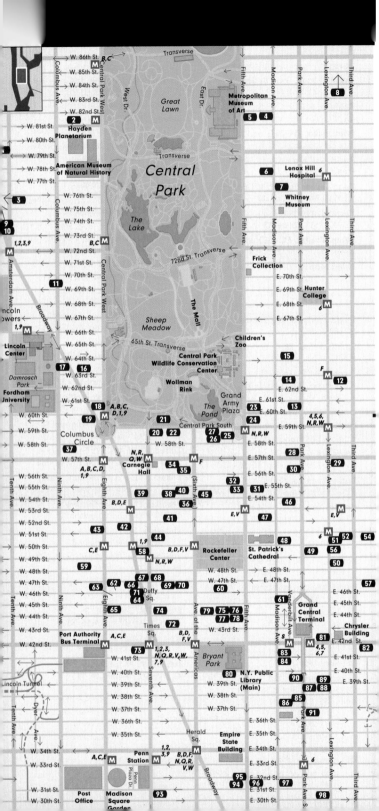

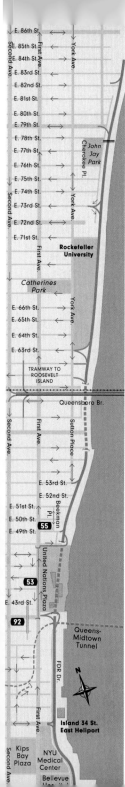

Listed by Site Number

Listed Alphabetically

Algonquin, 79. 59 W 44th St
☎ 840-6800. 🖷 944-1419. $$$

The Avalon, 96. 16 E 32nd St
☎ 299-7000. 🖷 299-7001. $$-$$$

Beekman Tower, 55. 3 Mitchell Pl
☎ 320-8018. 🖷 465-3697. $$-$$$

Belvedere Hotel, 59. 319 W 48th St
☎ 245-7000. 🖷 245-4455. $-$$

The Benjamin, 52. 125 E 50th St
☎ 715-2500. 🖷 715-2525. $$-$$$$

Broadway Inn Bed & Breakfast, 63.
264 W 46th St ☎ 997-9200.
🖷 768-2807. $-$$

The Bryant Park, 80. 40 W 40th St
☎ 869-0100. 🖷 869-4446. $$$-$$$$

Carlyle, 7. 35 E 76th St
☎ 744-1600. 🖷 717-5737. $$$$

Casablanca, 72. 147 W 43rd St
☎ 869-1212. 🖷 391-7585. $$

Central Park Intercontinental, 21.
112 Central Park S ☎ 757-1900.
🖷 757-9620. $$$

Chambers, 35. 15 W 56th St
☎ 974-5656. 🖷 974-5657. $$$

Crowne Plaza at the UN, 92.
304 E 42nd St ☎ 968-8800.
🖷 297-3440. $$$-$$$$

Doral Park Ave, 90. 70 Park Ave
☎ 687-7050. 🖷 973-2497. $$-$$$

Doubletree Guest Suites, 67. 1568 B'way
☎ 719-1600. 🖷 921-5212. $$-$$$

Drake Swissôtel, 30. 440 Park Ave
☎ 421-0900. 🖷 371-4190. $$$$

The Dylan, 84. 52 E 41st St
☎ 338-0500. 🖷 338-0569. $$$

Edison, 66. 228 W 47th St
☎ 840-5000. 🖷 596-6850. $-$$

Elysee, 46. 60 E 54th St
☎ 753-1066. 🖷 980-9278. $$$

Empire Hotel, 17. 44 W 63rd St
☎ 265-7400. 🖷 244-3382. $$

Essex House, 20. 160 Central Park S
☎ 247-0300. 🖷 315-1839. $$$

Excelsior, 2. 45 W 81st St
☎ 362-9200. 🖷 721-2994. $$

Fitzpatrick, 29. 687 Lexington Ave
☎ 355-0100. 🖷 355-1371. $$$

Flatotel, 41. 135 W 52nd St
☎ 887-9400. 🖷 887-9442. $$

Four Seasons, 28. 57 E 57th St
☎ 758-5700. 🖷 758-5711. $$$$

The Franklin, 8. 164 E 87th St
☎ 369-1000. 🖷 894-5220. $$$

Gorham, 40. 136 W 55th St
☎ 245-1800. 🖷 582-8332. $$-$$$$

Grand Hyatt NY, 81. Park Ave & 42nd
St ☎ 883-1234. 🖷 697-3772. $$-$$$

Helmsley Park Lane, 22. 36 Central
Park S ☎ 371-4000. 🖷 521-6666. $$$-$$$$

Herald Square Hotel, 94. 19 W 31st St
☎ 279-4017. 🖷 643-9208. $

Hilton Times Square, 73. 234 W 42nd
St ☎ 642-2500. 🖷 840-5516. $$$

Hotel Beacon, 11. 2130 B'way
☎ 787-1100. 🖷 787-8119. $$

Hotel Wales, 4. 1295 Madison Ave
☎ 876-6000. 🖷 860-7000. $$-$$$

Howard Johnson Plaza, 43. 851 Eighth
Ave ☎ 581-4100. 🖷 974-7502. $$

The Hudson, 37. 356 W 58th St
☎ 554-6000. 🖷 554-6001. $$-$$$$

The Iroquois, 76. 49 W 44th St
☎ 840-3080. 🖷 398-1754. $$$

Jolly Madison Towers, 85. 22 E 38th
St ☎ 802-0600. 🖷 447-0747. $$-$$$

Kitano, 87. 66 Park Ave
☎ 885-7000. 🖷 885-7100. $$$$

Le Parker Meridien, 34. 118 W 57th St
☎ 245-5000. 🖷 307-1776. $$$$

Library Hotel, 83. 299 Madison Ave
☎ 983-4500. 🖷 499-9099. $$$

Lowell, 14. 28 E 63rd St
☎ 838-1400. 🖷 605-6808. $$$$

Lucerne, 1. 201 W 79th St
☎ 875-1000. 🖷 721-1179. $$

Malibu Studios, 9. 2688 Broadway
☎ 222-2954. 🖷 678-6842. $

The Mansfield, 78. 12 W 44th St
☎ 944-6050. 🖷 764-4477. $$-$$$$

The Mark, 6. 25 E 77th St
☎ 744-4300. 🖷 472-5714. $$$$

Marriott Marquis, 64. 1535 B'way
☎ 398-1900. 🖷 704-8930. $$$$

Mayflower, 18. I5 Central Park W
☎ 265-0060. 🖷 265-0227. $$-$$$

Melrose Hotel, 12. 140 E 63rd St
☎ 838-5700. 🖷 223-3287. $$-$$$

Michelangelo, 44. 152 W 51st St
☎ 765-1900. 🖷 541-7618. $$$-$$$$

Milburn, 3. 242 W 76th St
☎ 362-1006. 🖷 721-5476. $$

Millennium Broadway, 74. 145 W
44th St ☎ 768-4400. 🖷 789-7688. $$

Millennium Hotel UN Plaza, 53.
1 UN Plaza ☎ 758-1234. 🖷 702-5051.
$$-$$$

Morgans, 86. 237 Madison Ave
☎ 686-0300. 🖷 779-8352. $$$

The Muse, 70. 130 W 46th St
☎ 485-2400. 🖷 485-2900. $$-$$$

NY Helmsley, 82. 212 E 42nd St
☎ 490-8900. 🖷 986-4792. $$-$$$

NY Hilton, 36. 1335 Sixth Ave
☎ 586-7000. 🖷 315-1374. $$-$$$$

NY Palace, 48. 455 Madison Ave
☎ 888-7000. 🖷 303-6000. $$$$

Novotel, 42. 226 W 52nd St
☎ 315-0100. 🖷 765-5369. $$

Omni Berkshire Place, 47. 21 E 52nd St
☎ 753-5800. 🖷 754-5020. $$$$

On The Ave, 10. 2177 Broadway
☎ 362-1100. 🖷 787-9521. $$

Paramount, 62. 235 W 46th St
☎ 764-5500. 🖷 354-5737. $$$-$$$$

The Peninsula, 33. 700 Fifth Ave
☎ 247-2200. 🖷 903-3943. $$$$

Pickwick Arms, 54. 230 E 51st St
☎ 355-0300. 🖷 755-5029. $

Pierre, 23. 2 E 61st St
☎ 838-8000. 🖷 758-1615. $$$$

The Plaza, 25. Fifth Ave & W 59th St
☎ 759-3000. 🖷 546-5324. $$-$$$$

Plaza Athénée, 15. 37 E 64th St
☎ 734-9100. 🖷 772-0958. $$$$

Plaza Fifty, 51. 155 E 50th St
☎ 751-5710. 🖷 753-1468. $$-$$$

Portland Square Hotel, 69. 132 W 47th St ☎ 382-0600. 🖷 382-0684. $

Quality Hotel and Suites, 60. 59 W 46th St ☎ 790-2710. 🖷 290-2760. $-$$

Quality Hotel East Side, 98. 161 Lexington Ave ☎ 545-1800. 🖷 481-7270. $$

Ramada Milford Plaza, 65. 270 W 45 St ☎ 869-3600 🖷 944-8357. $$

Red Roof Inn, 95. 6 W 32nd St
☎ 643-7100. 🖷 643-7101. $-$$

Regency, 13. 540 Park Ave
☎ 759-4100. 🖷 826-5674. $$$$

Renaissance, 68. 714 7th Ave
☎ 765-7676. 🖷 765-1962. $$$$

Rihga Royal, 38. 151 W 54th St
☎ 307-5000. 🖷 765-6530. $$$

Ritz-Carlton Central Park, 27. 50 Central Park S ☎ 308-9100. 🖷 207-8831. $$$$

Roger Smith, 50. 501 Lexington Ave ☎ 755-1400. 🖷 758-4061. $$

Roger Williams, 97. 131 Madison Ave ☎ 448-7000. 🖷 448-7007. $$

Roosevelt, 61. 45 E 45th St
☎ 661-9600. 🖷 885-6162. $$

Royalton, 77. 44 W 44th St
☎ 869-4400. 🖷 575-0012. $$$-$$$$

St Regis, 31. 2 E 55th St
☎ 753-4500. 🖷 787-3447. $$$$

Sheraton Russell, 91. 45 Park Ave
☎ 685-7676. 🖷 889-3193. $$-$$$$

Sherry Netherland, 24. 781 Fifth Ave
☎ 355-2800. 🖷 319-4306. $$$-$$$$

Shoreham, 32. 33 W 55th St
☎ 247-6700. 🖷 765-9741. $$

Sofitel New York, 75. 45 W 44th St
☎ 354-8844. 🖷 782-3002. $$-$$$$

Southgate Tower, 93. 371 Seventh Ave
☎ 320-8050. 🖷 714-2159. $$

Stanhope Park Hyatt, 5. 995 Fifth Ave
☎ 774-1234. 🖷 517-0088. $$$-$$$$

The Time, 58. 224 W 49th St
☎ 320-2900. 🖷 245-2305. $$$

Trump International Hotel & Towers, 19. 1 Central Park West
☎ 299-1000. 🖷 299-1150.

Vanderbilt YMCA, 57. 224 E 47th St
☎ 756-9600. 🖷 752-0210. $

W New York, 56. 541 Lexington Ave
☎ 755-1200. 🖷 319-8344. $$-$$$$

W New York—The Court, 88. 130 E 39th St ☎ 685-1100. 🖷 889-0287. $$-$$$$

W New York—Tuscany, 89. 120 E 39th St ☎ 779-7822. 🖷 696-2095. $$-$$$$

W Times Square, 71. 1567 Broadway
☎ 930-7400. 🖷 930-7500. $$$

Waldorf–Astoria, 49. 301 Park Ave
☎ 355-3000. 🖷 872-7272. $$$$

Warwick, 45. 65 W 54th St
☎ 247-2700. 🖷 713-1751. $$$

Wellington, 39. 871 Seventh Ave
☎ 247-3900. 🖷 581-1719. $$

West Side YMCA, 16. 5 W 63rd St
☎ 875-4100. 🖷 875-1334. $

Wyndham, 26. 42 W 58th St
☎ 753-3500. 🖷 754-5638. $-$$

$$$$ = *over $400* $$$ = *$275–$400* $$ = *$150–$275* $ = *under $150*

All prices are for a standard double room, excluding 13¼% city and state sales tax and $2 occupancy tax.

Listed by Site Number

Listed Alphabetically

Best Western Seaport Inn, 29.
33 Peck Slip ☎ 766-6600.
📠 766-6615. $$

Carlton Arms, 8. 160 E 25th St
☎ 684-8337. $

Chelsea Inn, 16. 46 W 17th St
☎ 645-8989. 📠 645-1903. $

Chelsea Lodge, 14. 318 W 20th St
☎ 243-4499. 📠 243-7852. $-$$

Chelsea Pines Inn, 15. 317 W 14th St
☎ 929-1023. 📠 620-5646. $

Chelsea Savoy, 2. 204 W 23rd St
☎ 929-9353. 📠 741-6309. $-$$

Chelsea Star Hotel, 1. 300 W 30th St
☎ 244-7827. 📠 279-9018. $

Colonial House Inn, 13.
318 W 22nd St ☎ 243-9669. $

Cosmopolitan, 26. 95 W Broadway
☎ 566-1900. 📠 566-6909. $-$$

Embassy Suites Hotel, 27.
102 North End Ave ☎ 945-0100.
📠 945-3012. $$-$$$$

The Gershwin, 5. 7 E 27th St
☎ 545-8000. 📠 684-5546. $

The Giraffe, 6. 365 Park Ave S
☎ 685-7700. 📠 685-7771. $$$

Gramercy Park Hotel, 9.
2 Lexington Ave ☎ 475-4320.
📠 205-0535. $$

Holiday Inn Downtown, 24.
138 Lafayette St ☎ 966-8898.
📠 966-3933. $-$$

Holiday Inn Wall Street, 31.
15 Gold St ☎ 232-7700. 📠 425-0330.
$$-$$$

Hotel 17, 12. 225 E 17th St
☎ 475-2845. 📠 677-8178. $

Inn at Irving Place, 10. 56 Irving Pl
☎ 533-4600. 📠 533-4611. $$$-$$$$

Inn on 23rd, 3. 131 W 23rd St
☎ 463-0330. 📠 463-0302. $$

La Semana Hotel, 4. 25 W 24th St
☎ 255-5944. 📠 675-3830. $

Larchmont Hotel, 17. 27 W 11th St
☎ 989-9333. 📠 989-9496. $

Mercer Hotel, 22. 147 Mercer St
☎ 966-6060. 📠 965-3838. $$$

Millennium Hilton, 28. 55 Church St
☎ 693-2001. 📠 571-2317.
(re-opening Fall 2003) $$$-$$$$

**New York City Howard
Johnson, 20.**
135 E Houston St ☎ 358-8844.
📠 473-3500. $

NY Marriott Brooklyn, 34.
333 Adams St ☎ 718/246-7000.
📠 718/246-0563. $$

Park South Hotel, 7. 122 E 28th St
☎ 448-0888. 📠 448-0811. $$

Regent Wall Street, 30. 55 Wall St
☎ 845-8600. 📠 845-8601. $$$$

Ritz-Carlton Battery Park, 32.
2 West St ☎ 344-0800. 📠 344-3801.
$$$-$$$$

St Mark's Hotel, 19. 2 St Marks Pl
☎ 674-2192 $

60 Thompson, 21. 60 Thompson St
☎ 431-0400. 📠 431-0200. $$$$

SoHo Grand, 23. 310 W Broadway
☎ 965-3000 📠 965-3244. $$$-$$$$

Tribeca Grand, 25. 2 Sixth Ave
☎ 519-6600. 📠 519-6700. $$-$$$

W-Union Square, 11. 201 Park Ave S
☎ 253-9119. 📠 779-0148. $$-$$$$

Wall Street Inn, 33.
9 William St ☎ 747-1500. 📠 747-1900.
$$$

Washington Square Hotel, 18.
103 Waverly Pl ☎ 777-9515.
📠 979-8373. $-$$

$$$$ = *over $400* $$$ = *$275-$400* $$ = *$150-$275* $ = *under $150*
*All prices are for a standard double room, excluding 13¼% city and state sales tax
and $2 occupancy tax.*

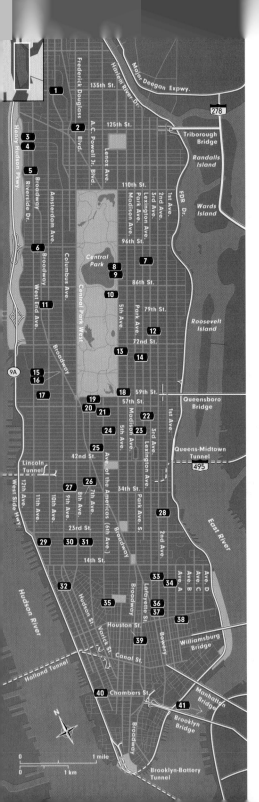

Listed Alphabetically

Aaron Davis Hall, 1.
135 Convent Ave ☎ 650-7100

Amato Opera, 37.
319 Bowery ☎ 228-8200

Angel Orensanz Foundation, 38.
172 Norfolk St ☎ 529-7194

Apollo Theater, 2.
253 W 125th St ☎ 749-5838

Beacon Theater, 11.
2124 Broadway ☎ 496-7070

Brooklyn Academy of Music, 41.
30 Lafayette Ave ☎ 718/636-4100

CAMI Hall, 19.
165 W 57th St ☎ 841-9650

Carnegie Hall, 20.
154 W 57th St ☎ 247-7800

Church of the Heavenly Rest, 8.
2 E 90th St ☎ 289-3400

City Center, 21.
131 W 55th St ☎ 581-1212

Cunningham Studio, 32.
55 Bethune St ☎ 691-9751

Dance Theatre Workshop, 32.
219 W 19th St from fall 2002
☎ 924-0077

DiCapo Opera Theater, 12.
184 E 76th St ☎ 288-9438

Dixon Place at Vineyard 26, 28.
309 E 26th St ☎ 532-1546

Florence Gould Hall, 18.
55 E 59th St ☎ 355-6160

Frick Museum, 13.
1 E 70th St ☎ 288-0700

Guggenheim Museum, 9.
1071 Fifth Ave ☎ 423-3500

Hammerstein Ballroom, 27.
311 W 34th St ☎ 485-1534

John Jay Theater, 17.
899 Tenth Ave ☎ 237-8000

Joyce SoHo, 38.
155 Mercer St ☎ 334-7479

Joyce Theater, 31.
175 Eighth Ave ☎ 242-0800

Kaye Playhouse, 14.
695 Park Ave ☎ 772-4448

The Kitchen, 30.
512 W 19th St ☎ 255-5793

La MaMa ETC, 36.
74A E 4th St ☎ 254-6468

Lincoln Center, 16.
Broadway & 64th St
☎ 875-5000
·Alice Tully Hall ☎ 721-6500
·Avery Fisher Hall ☎ 875-5030
·Juilliard Theatre ☎ 769-7406
·Metropolitan Opera ☎ 362-6000
·NY State Theater ☎ 870-5570

Madison Square Garden, 26.
Seventh Ave & 32nd St ☎ 465-6741

Manhattan School of Music, 3.
120 Claremont Ave ☎ 749-2802

Merkin Concert Hall, 17.
129 W 67th St ☎ 501-3330

Metropolitan Museum, 10.
1000 Fifth Ave ☎ 879-5500

Miller Theater, 5. Columbia Univ,
Broadway & W 116th St ☎ 854-7799

92nd St Y, 7.
1395 Lexington Ave ☎ 415-5580

PS 122, 34.
150 First Ave ☎ 477-5288

Radio City Music Hall, 24.
1260 Sixth Ave ☎ 247-4777

Riverside Church, 4.
91 Claremont Ave ☎ 870-6700

St Bartholomew's Church, 23.
109 E 50th St ☎ 378-0200

St Mark's-in-the-Bowery, 33.
Second Ave & 10th St ☎ 674-6377

St Peter's Church, 22.
619 Lexington Ave ☎ 935-2200

Symphony Space, 6.
2537 Broadway ☎ 864-5400

Town Hall, 25.
123 W 43rd St ☎ 997-1003

**TriBeCa Performing Arts
Center, 39.** 199 Chambers St
☎ 346-8510

Washington Square Church, 35.
135 W 4th St ☎ 777-2528

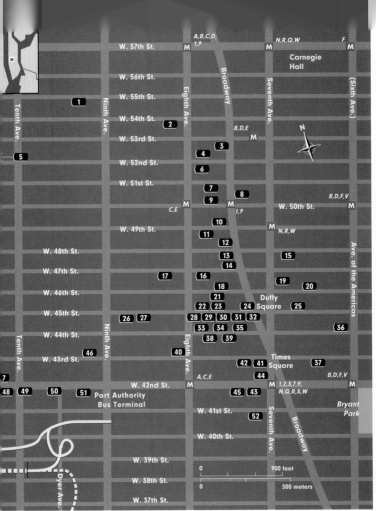

Listed by Site Number

Listed Alphabetically

Ambassador, 10. 215 W 49th St
☎ 239-6200

American Airlines, 42. 227 W 42nd St
☎ 719-1300

American Place, 20. 111 W 46th St
☎ 239-6200

American Theatre of Actors, 2.
314 W 54th St ☎ 206-1515

Belasco, 36. 111 W 44th St
☎ 239-6200

Booth, 31. 222 W 45th St ☎ 239-6200

Broadhurst, 34. 235 W 44th St
☎ 239-6200

Broadway, 3. 1681 Broadway
☎ 239-6200

Brooks Atkinson, 16. 256 W 47th St
☎ 307-4100

Circle in the Square, 9.
1633 Broadway ☎ 239-6200

Cort, 15. 138 W 48th St ☎ 239-6200

Douglas Fairbanks, 50.
432 W 42nd St ☎ 239-6200

The Duke, 45. 229 W 42nd St
☎ 239-6200

Ensemble Studio Theatre, 5.
549 W 52nd St ☎ 247-3405

Ethel Barrymore, 14. 243 W 47th St
☎ 239-6200

Eugene O'Neill, 11. 230 W 49th St
☎ 239-6200

**Ford Center for the Performing Arts,
41.** 214 W 43rd St ☎ 307-4100

47th St, 17. 304 W 47th St ☎ 239-6200

Gershwin, 7. 222 W 51st St
☎ 307-4100

Golden, 28. 252 W 45th St
☎ 239-6200

Helen Hayes, 39. 240 W 44th St
☎ 239-6200

Henry Miller's, 37. 124 W 43rd St
☎ 239-6200

Imperial, 22. 249 W 45th St
☎ 239-6200

John Houseman, 49. 450 W 42nd St
☎ 967-9077

José Quintero, 48. 534 W 42nd St
☎ 563-1684

Longacre, 13. 220 W 48th St
☎ 239-6200

Lunt-Fontanne, 18. 205 W 46th St
☎ 307-4747

Lyceum, 25. 149 W 45th St
☎ 239-6200

Majestic, 33. 247 W 44th St
☎ 239-6200

Marquis, 24. 1535 Broadway
☎ 307-4100

Martin Beck, 27. 302 W 45th St
☎ 239-6200

Minskoff, 32. 200 W 45th St
☎ 869-0550

Music Box, 23. 239 W 45th St
☎ 239-6200

Nederlander, 52. 208 W 41st St
☎ 307-4100

Neil Simon, 6. 250 W 52nd St
☎ 307-4100

New Amsterdam, 43. 214 W 42nd St
☎ 307-4747

New Victory, 44. 209 W 42nd St
☎ 236-6200

Palace, 19. 1554 Broadway
☎ 307-4747

Playwrights Horizons, 51.
416 W 42nd St ☎ 279-4200

Plymouth, 30. 236 W 45th St
☎ 239-6200

Primary Stages, 26. 354 W 45th St
☎ 333-4052

Richard Rogers, 21. 226 W 46th St
☎ 307-4100

Royale, 29. 242 W 45th St
☎ 239-6200

St James, 38. 246 W 44th St
☎ 239-6200

Second Stage, 40. 307 W 43rd St
☎ 246-4422

Shubert, 35. 225 W 44th St
☎ 239-6200

Signature Theater, 47.
555 W 42nd St ☎ 244-7529

Theatre Four, 1. 424 W 55th St
☎ 239-6200

Virginia, 4. 245 W 52nd St
☎ 239-6200

Walter Kerr, 12. 219 W 48th St
☎ 239-6200

Westside Theatre, 46.
407 W 43rd St ☎ 239-6200

Winter Garden, 8.
1634 Broadway ☎ 563-5544

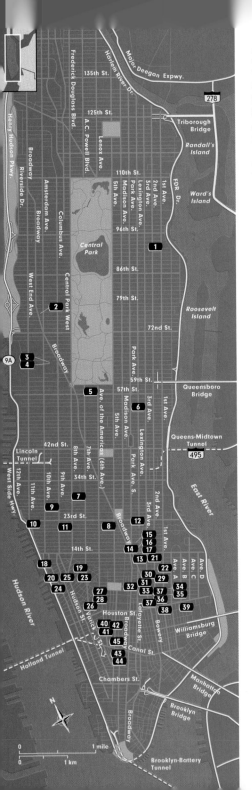

Listed Alphabetically

Actor's Playhouse, 23.
100 Seventh Ave S ☎ 463-0060

Arthur's Dress Shop, 39.
141 Ridge St ☎ 420-8877

Astor Place, 32.
434 Lafayette St ☎ 254-4370

Atlantic Theater Company, 11.
336 W 20th St ☎ 239-6200

Bank Street, 20.
155 Bank St ☎ 561-9635

Century Center, 16.
111 E 15th St ☎ 239-6200

Cherry Lane, 26.
38 Commerce St ☎ 239-6200

Classic Stage Company, 20.
136 E 13th St ☎ 677-4210

Culture Project, 37.
45 Bleeker St ☎ 420-8877

Daryl Roth Theatre, 14.
20 Union Sq E ☎ 239-6200

East Thirteenth Street, 13.
136 E 13th St ☎ 239-6200

Flea Theatre, 44.
41 White St ☎ 226-0051

Gramercy Theatre, 12.
127 E 23rd St ☎ 307-4100

HERE, 41. 145 Sixth Ave ☎ 647-0202

Hudson Guild, 9.
441 W 26th St ☎ 206-1515

Irish Repertory Theatre, 8.
132 W 22nd St ☎ 727-2737

Jane Street, 18.
113 Jane St ☎ 239-6200

Jean Cocteau Rep, 36.
330 Bowery ☎ 677-0060

Kraine, 35. 85 E 4th St ☎ 420-8877

La MaMa ETC, 34.
74A E 4th St ☎ 475-7710

Lucille Lortel, 25.
121 Christopher St ☎ 627-7373

Manhattan Theatre Club, 5.
131 W 55th St ☎ 581-1212

McGinn/Cazale, 2.
2162 Broadway ☎ 307-4100

Minetta Lane, 28.
18 Minetta La ☎ 307-4100

Mitzi Newhouse, 3.
Lincoln Center, 150 W 65th St
☎ 239-6200

New York Theatre Workshop, 33.
79 E 4th St ☎ 460-5475

Ohio, 42. 66 Wooster St ☎ 966-4844

Orpheum, 29.
126 Second Ave ☎ 477-2477

Pearl Theatre Co, Inc, 30.
80 St Marks Pl ☎ 598-9802

Performing Garage, 42.
33 Wooster St ☎ 966-3651

Players, 27.
115 MacDougal St ☎ 254-5076

Playhouse 91, 1.
316 E 91st St ☎ 307-4100

Promenade, 2.
2162 Broadway ☎ 239-6200

Public, 31.
425 Lafayette St ☎ 673-7030

Rattlestick Theatre, 19.
224 Waverly Pl ☎ 627-2556

Sanford Meisner, 10.
164 Eleventh Ave ☎ 206-1764

SoHo Playhouse, 40.
15 Vandam St ☎ 239-6200

SoHo Rep, 43.
46 Walker St ☎ 414-5136

Surf Reality, 38.
172 Allen St ☎ 465-3410

Theater for the New City, 22.
155 First Ave ☎ 420-8877

29th St Rep, 7.
212 W 29th St ☎ 206-1515

Union Square Theatre, 15.
100 E 17th St ☎ 505-0700

Variety Arts Theatre, 21.
110 Third Ave ☎ 239-6200

Vineyard Theatre, 17.
108 E 15th St ☎ 353-0303

Vivian Beaumont, 4.
Lincoln Center, Broadway
& W 64th St ☎ 362-7600

Wings Theater, 24.
154 Christopher St ☎ 627-2961

York, 6.
619 Lexington Ave ☎ 239-6200

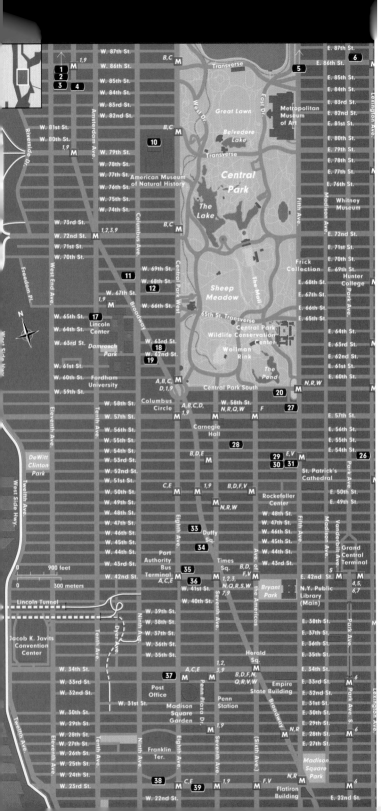

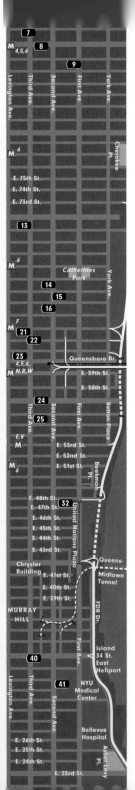

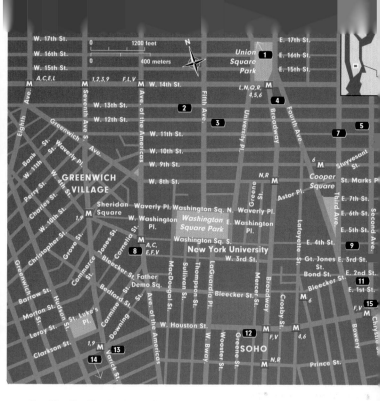

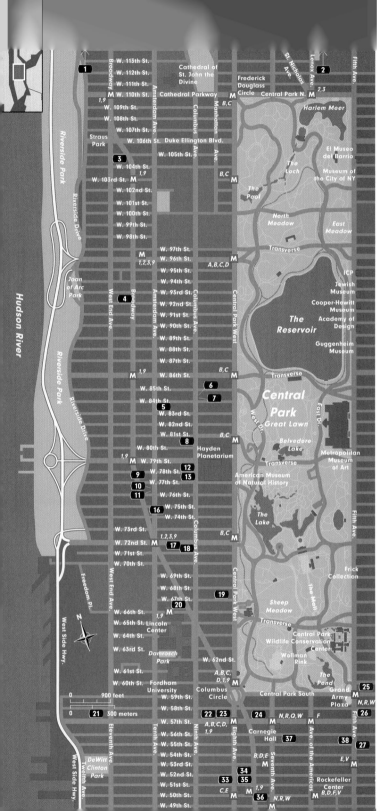

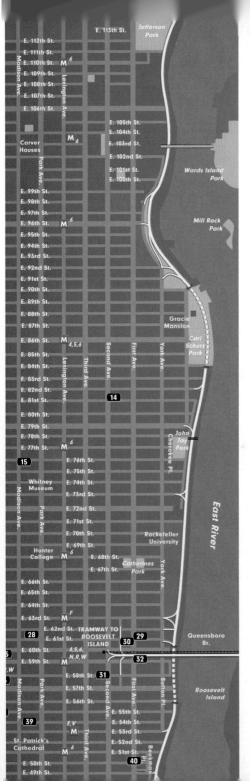

Listed by Site Number (cont.)

Listed Alphabetically

Monkey Bar, 39. 60 E 54th St
☎ 838-2600. Bar

The Monster, 123. 80 Grove St
☎ 924-3557. Gay/Disco

Nell's, 85. 246 W 14th St
☎ 675-1567. Dance Club

New York Comedy Club, 64.
241 E 24th St ☎ 696-5233. Comedy

Nuyorican Poets Cafe, 110.
236 E 3rd St ☎ 505-8183.
Spoken Word

Ohm, 73. 16 W 22nd St
☎ 229-2000. Dance Club

Old Town Bar, 87. 45 E 18th St
☎ 529-6732. Bar

169 Bar, 154. 169 E Broadway
☎ 473-8866. Dance Club

Pen Top, 38. Peninsula Hotel,
700 Fifth Ave ☎ 247-2200. Bar

Pete's Tavern, 86. 129 E 18th St
☎ 473-7676. Bar

Polly Esther's, 129. 179 Varick St
☎ 243-1999. Dance Club

Potion Lounge, 13. 370 Columbus Ave
☎ 721-4386. Nightclub

Pravda, 143. 281 Lafayette St
☎ 226-4696. Bar

Prohibition, 7. 503 Columbus Ave
☎ 579-3100. Funk/Jazz

Red Blazer, 60. 32 W 37th St
☎ 947-6428. Jazz/Blues/Swing

Remedy Lounge, 75. 36 E 20th St
☎ 674-4596. Bar

Rodeo Bar, 62. 375 Third Ave
☎ 683-6500.
Country/Rockabilly/Blues

Roseland, 34. 239 W 52nd St
☎ 247-0200. Ballroom/Rock

Rose's Turn, 126. 55 Grove St
☎ 366-5438. Cabaret

Roxy, 77. 515 W 18th St
☎ 645-5156. Dance Club

Royalton Bar, 54. 44 W 44th St
☎ 869-4400. Bar

Sardi's, 57. 234 W 44th St
☎ 221-8444. Bar

SBNY, 88. 50 W 17th St
☎ 691-0073. Gay

Shark Bar, 16. 307 Amsterdam Ave
☎ 874-8500. Bar

Shine, 151. 285 W Broadway
☎ 941-0900. Rock/Dance

Smalls, 102. 183 W 10th St
☎ 929-7565. Jazz

Smoke, 3. 2751 Broadway
☎ 864-6662. Jazz

SOB's, 130. 204 Varick St
☎ 243-4940. Brazilian/Reggae/Jazz

Sound Factory, 42. 618 W 46th St
☎ 489-0001. Dance Club

Spa, 97. 76 E 13th St
☎ 388-1060. Dance Club

Stand Up NY, 9. 236 W 78th St
☎ 595-0850. Comedy

Supper Club, 49. 240 W 47th St
☎ 921-1940. Cabaret

Surf Reality, 134. 172 Allen St
☎ 673-4182. Comedy

Swing 46, 46. 349 W 46th St
☎ 262-9554. Swing

Temple Bar, 132. 332 Lafayette St
☎ 925-4242. Bar

Terra Blues, 120. 149 Bleecker St
☎ 777-7776. Blues

Tiki Room, 74. 4 W 22nd St
☎ 646/230-1444. Bar/Lounge

Tonic, 140. 107 Norfolk St
☎ 358-7503. Jazz/Eclectic

Top of the Tower, 52. 3 Mitchell Pl
☎ 355-7300. Bar

Townhouse, 31. 236 E 58th St
☎ 754-4649. Gay

Triad, 17. 158 W 72nd St ☎ 362-2590.
Cabaret

Twirl, 69. 208 W 23rd St
☎ 691-7685. Gay/Dance Club

Village Underground, 117.
130 W 3rd St ☎ 777-7745. Rock

Village Vanguard, 98.
178 Seventh Ave S ☎ 255-4037.
Jazz/Blues

Webster Hall, 96. 125 E 11th St
☎ 353-1600. Dance Club

Westside Brewery, 10.
340 Amsterdam Ave ☎ 721-2161. Bar

White Horse Tavern, 101.
567 Hudson St ☎ 989-3956. Bar

The Works, 8. 428 Columbus Ave
☎ 799-7365. Gay

xl, 81. 357 W 16th St ☎ 995-1400. Gay

Zinc Bar, 131. 90 W Houston St
☎ 477-8337. Jazz